UFOs and the extraterrestrial MESSAGE

Other titles by Richard Lawrence

Prayer Energy

Gods, Guides and Guardian Angels

Unlock your Psychic Powers

Contacts with the Gods from Space (co-authored with Dr George King)

Realise Your Inner Potential (co-authored with Dr George King)

The Meditation Plan

Little Book of Karma

The Magic of Healing

UFOs and the extraterrestrial MESSAGE

A spiritual insight into UFOs and cosmic transmissions

Richard Lawrence

CICO BOOKS

LONDON NEW YORK

Published in 2010 by CICO Books

An imprint of Ryland Peters & Small

20–21 Jockey's Fields
London WC1R 4BW

519 Broadway, 5th Floor
New York NY 10012

www.cicobooks.com

10 9 8 7 6 5 4 3 2 1

ISBN 978 1 907030 15 4

Printed in the UK by CPI William Clowes Beccles NR34 7TL

Editor: Marion Paull
Designer: Jerry Goldie

CONTENTS

ACKNOWLEDGMENTS

T his book would not have been written without the invaluable help of several people to all of whom I am very grateful. UFO expert Ananda Sirisena drew on his considerable knowledge of UFOs, encounters, and attempted government cover-ups to provide comprehensive research for the early chapters. Award-winning journalist Hazel Courteney guided me through some of the cutting-edge discoveries of the new science and shared her research generously with me. My wife, Alyson, has been a fount of knowledge about western mysticism upon which she has lectured widely. Author and former personal assistant to Dr George King, Brian Keneipp, provided in-depth details about the transmissions received by Dr King as well as a wonderful selection for this book. Nikki Perrott and Noémi Perkin worked tirelessly in transcribing, correcting, checking, and researching material for this book and in doing so played an essential part in its composition. I would also like to thank Dr John Holder, Lesley Young, Mark Bennett, and Bryan Craig for their significant contribution to the book in various ways. My special thanks go to the International Directors of The Aetherius Society for their enthusiasm for this project from its inception, for the input they have given me, and for giving permission for the inclusion of extensive passages from Aetherius Society publications. Above all, I wish to thank my spiritual teacher, Dr George King, without whom I would not have discovered the truth about UFOs and the extraterrestrial message, never mind written a book about it.

INTRODUCTION

Thousands of years ago, three men looked into the night sky and saw a bright light moving above them. These men, steeped in the learning of the day, understood astronomy and astrology as compatible sciences, and were not easily fooled or subject to delusion or wishful thinking. Much as the object they were viewing looked like a star, they knew that it couldn't be, because it was clearly moving—and in a specific direction.

Today, you can look up at the sky, see a moving object, and wonder whether it could be a satellite, an aircraft, a weather balloon, or some other terrestrial object. No such inventions had been made then. Meteorites, seen as shooting stars, would flash across the sky and disappear, but they wouldn't follow a deliberate flight path. Comets, suns, and planets were too far distant for their movements to pinpoint a particular location on Earth—especially for men using the naked eye, and who were probably riding on camels, to find what they were looking for.

According to an ancient account, which was first passed down orally and later recorded in writing, these men followed the light until it stopped over a building. The account indicates that they were on a quest and that this sighting had a profound and uplifting effect upon them. Sure enough, in the very building over which the light had stopped, they found exactly what they had been seeking.

They were, of course, the three wise men, the moving object was the Star of Bethlehem, and the focus of their search was Jesus Christ. To quote from the book of Matthew, chapter 2, verses 9–11:

9 When they had heard the King, they departed: and lo, the star, which they saw in the east, went before them, till it came and stood over where the young child was.

10 When they saw the star, they rejoiced with exceeding great joy.

11   And when they were come into the house, they saw the young child with Mary his
mother, and fell down, and worshipped him: and when they had opened their
treasures, they presented unto him gifts; gold, and frankincense, and myrrh.

Philo, a Jewish Platonist who commentated on the Hebrew scriptures and was a contemporary of Jesus's, wrote that among the Persians there was an Order of the Magi who "silently made research into the fruits of nature to gain knowledge of the truth." He said that through visions clearer than speech they gave and received revelations of divine excellency. This suggests that they were mystics who cultivated their own inner realizations as a path to wisdom. It is generally believed that the wise men of the story were Persian priests, possibly Zoroastrians, and it may be significant that the Zoroastrians, like the Jews, believed in a messiah who would descend from heaven. Some scholars believe there may have been considerably more than three, and that the only reason they went down in history as three wise men was because the gifts they brought were three in number, namely gold, frankincense, and myrrh.

Many attempts have been made to identify the Star of Bethlehem as an astronomical object. Explanations by astronomers and other scientists range from its being Jupiter to a comet to a supernova, but none of these could explain how this moving object "stood over where the young child was." Even if there was an unusual alignment of planets or some other exceptional astronomical event around the time of Jesus's birth, it would not explain the event related in St Matthew's gospel.

Two thousand years later, on July 23 1958, on a hill overlooking the ocean, a lone Englishman was seated in a yogic posture, praying for peace in the world. Dimly, out of the corner of his eye, he saw a bright blue sphere skipping across the night sky. It stopped dead in its tracks over the sea before him and hovered. He continued to pray.

After a few minutes, he became aware of the same being that the wise men had seen so long ago, standing just a few yards away from him, but this time not in swaddling clothes. He stood tall, radiant, and dressed from the shoulders to the ground in a robe that seemed to glow with a bluish-white incandescence. The Master Jesus had come to Holdstone Down, near Combe Martin in Devon, England, to charge it with spiritual power through the channel he had chosen for this task, the yoga master Dr George King. It was to become one of the holy mountains of the world. When the operation was complete, Dr King described the departure of this godlike being:

He fixed me with a penetrating but kindly gaze for a moment, then a wide beam of green light sprang out of a faintly luminous shape hovering above the ground, about thirty yards away. The Master Jesus moved a few steps to one side, into this beam—and was gone ...

High up in the heavens I saw two bluish spheres of light, like two bright, unblinking stars. They were joined by a third which came upwards to meet them. Then these three spacecraft travelled quickly across the skies to disappear over the western horizon. I knew that He had returned to the cosmos and my mission was completed.

Fifty years later, on July 26 2008, more than 130 pilgrims to Holdstone Down commemorated this extraordinary event by sending prayers of thankfulness to great extraterrestrial beings. Within hours, one of the biggest spates of UFO sightings occurred in various parts of the British Isles, as reported in the national press for several days. The *Sun* reported that a "record number of UFO sightings up and down the country on Saturday night has baffled experts. Mysterious objects spotted included bright orange balls shooting through the sky and strange flickering lights." The *North Devon Gazette* of Wednesday, July 30 devoted its front page to a sighting that took place ten miles away in South Molton, just a few hours after the pilgrimage. A family sitting in their garden at around 10 p.m. saw an object coming toward them. As they watched, it slowed down, moved above their house, and then shot up at a 40-degree angle at great speed, until it disappeared among the stars. Not much farther away, in Barnstaple, two objects were reported, and sightings occurred in many other parts of the UK that night, including Bedfordshire, Manchester, Leicester, Wakefield, Goring, and Basingstoke.

I was privileged to lead this pilgrimage of members and friends of The Aetherius Society, and appeared on several radio stations discussing the link between UFOs and spirituality. This link, I believe, is the key to the most important phenomenon of our time. As the Society's executive secretary for Europe for over thirty years, I have witnessed the spiritual impact of our cosmic visitors on many occasions, and can vouch for its authenticity from personal experience. The Aetherius Society is a worldwide spiritual organization founded by Dr King in 1955 to spread the truth about extraterrestrial beings and their message to our world. More important even than the message is the fact that the Society cooperates directly with these intelligences in a variety of ways for the betterment of humanity as a whole. Although this may sound very strange to some readers, I hope that by the time you have read this book you will detect the ring of truth behind these words.

One of the strange psychological quirks of human beings is that we seem to find it very difficult to believe in extraordinary events that happen in our own lifetimes. It is perfectly acceptable for those of religious faith to believe in the parting of the Red Sea at the time of Moses, the divine powers and manifestations connected with Sri Krishna in a bygone age, or the virgin birth and resurrection of Jesus Christ two thousand years ago, but the occurrence of spiritual events of such magnitude in these days is altogether a different matter.

The passage of time, and the many generations who have held firmly to a belief in these events, makes them much easier to accept. To think that such things are happening now is somehow more disturbing, even threatening to some, and yet, logically, there is no reason why great spiritual happenings should be restricted to the past. On the contrary, the unprecedented challenges that face our world today suggest that never has divine intervention been more necessary. In my view, extraterrestrial spacecraft and the message they bring are more needed now than they have ever been.

Just as people find it easier to accept great happenings from the distant past than they do from the present, so they can often deal more easily with the truth of paranormal events through the medium of fiction than when it is presented as a documented fact. Fiction, although it may contain many elements of truth, always provides us with an "out" because we know that it is made up. Contemporary factual incidents impinge on our reality, our grasp of the truth. When they are not softened through the medium of fiction, there is no middle ground. We have to either accept or reject them.

If ever we needed the help of the gods, the Cosmic Masters, call them what you will, it is surely now. After all, we are facing dire warnings on the ecological front; we have the capacity to destroy ourselves for the first time in this civilization; mass overpopulation is a problem; as many conflicts as ever are raging, with far more deadly weapons to carry them out; and we are up against a new kind of terrorism, not to mention poverty on a gigantic scale. Why should we be scouring old records for evidence of miraculous happenings, of intervention from above, or escaping into the world of fiction to grapple with extraordinary events, when by any reckoning they should be happening now?

4

And why is it that those who are religious, for the most part, follow their parents' creed? There is no reason to suppose that, because you are born into a particular faith, it is the truest and most effective path for you to follow to God. You would not necessarily take up the profession of your father or mother, so why take up their religion? Is it that people can't be bothered to investigate any other beliefs? Would it be too inconvenient if they found them to be true? Or is it out of fear?

Is this inability to deal with what's going on now also the reason for the gigantic cover-up of what governments consider to be unpalatable truths about UFOs? And yet, despite the numerous attempts to debunk them over the years by governments, the media, and skeptical organizations, UFOs keep on being seen by people from all walks of life, all over the world. Every now and then, someone thinks they have disproved them. Some go further and declare the phenomenon dead. Then, sure enough, a whole new spate of sightings occurs to resuscitate it. A so-called expert tries to explain why UFOs don't exist, but all too often people have less faith in the explanation than they do in the phenomenon itself.

In the meantime, governments have poured money into space programs—money that could have been used to save thousands of lives much closer to home here on Earth. Advanced telescopes are focused far into unknown regions of the galaxy in the hopes of finding planets that can sustain life, but should we find them, no one has any firm idea how to make contact with their inhabitants. The technology to visit these planets does not exist, despite current attempts to develop it—and none of this highly costly research relates convincingly to life that, to coin the "Star Trek" phrase, is "not as we know it."

Then there are the scaremongers, some of whom have been employed by governments, who deliberately propagate fear. What if they invade? How will we defend ourselves against them? There is a simple answer to that: we won't. Not just because we couldn't possibly do so, but also thankfully because we won't need to since, fortunately for us, they are not hostile. If they were, we would certainly know about it by now. Among the more sinister ideas that are put about from time to time to sow seeds of fear and hostility is the notion that they come to mutilate our cattle. According to this theory, technologically advanced beings use their vehicles to travel millions of miles to another world, using a science so sophisticated as to be beyond our comprehension, because they have a sadistic interest in alien livestock. This type of theory doesn't deserve a response, except to say that UFOs are here for far more elevated purposes than this, as I will try to demonstrate in this book.

Abduction is another controversial subject. Of course, we should all keep an open mind, and anyone who has investigated this phenomenon must conclude that something paranormal is going on in certain abduction cases. However, alien beings who have the ability to travel through space at fantastic velocities while nurturing an unhealthy desire to perform strange operations on individuals from another race, would not need to abduct people from their beds and take them to their craft to insert strange implants into them, as some claim. If that was the case, they could easily take over all the hospitals of the world, performing surgery to their heart's content and inserting implants like there was no tomorrow.

Again, I have to reject this theory for a far nobler concept of our alien visitors. Some abduction cases should be taken seriously, though, and not put down to an overactive imagination. Fascinating encounters with alien beings who are far from hostile have been reported, for example, and some people may be subject to psychic interference, which they mistakenly identify as otherworldly. As Shakespeare's Hamlet put it, "There are more things in heaven and earth, Horatio, than are dreamt of in your philosophy." Whereas in Shakespearean England a paranormal phenomenon might be seen as witchcraft or a ghostly body, today it is very often identified with aliens when it might have absolutely nothing to do with them whatsoever. The only conclusion an open-minded researcher can come to, in my view, is that there is a plan behind the UFO phenomenon—a grandiose, cosmic plan that is, at the same time, extremely subtle and certainly benign. If it wasn't, you wouldn't be reading this book and I wouldn't have been able to write it. It would all have been over a long, long time ago.

This book is not intended to be a compilation of UFO sightings throughout the ages from different geographical regions and cultures. You can easily find that on the internet or in any number of publications. Once it is established that they have been sighted throughout history— from cave drawings, ancient religious texts, indigenous tribal accounts, and Egyptian hieroglyphs to medieval European monastic records, the modern media, and much more in between—just repeating accounts of UFO sightings can become almost tedious. I was quoted once in London's *Time Out* as saying that, after a while, UFO-spotting can become a cosmic form of train-spotting. That was not meant to be disrespectful to our cosmic visitors. The point I was trying to make was that just banging on about UFO sightings can miss the point—namely, why they are here.

Another thing this book is not is a definitive account of government cover-ups and conspiracy theories about the concealment of UFO information by official bodies. The facts about UFO sightings through the ages, and modern-day attempts by governments to hide them, are both vital aspects of this subject and will be referred to extensively, but only if they help to answer the important questions about UFOs.

So, while this book will not be a new, exhaustive catalog of UFO data, it will deal with the all-important issue of their plan for our world. What kind of beings are these? Will they ever land openly among us for all to see, and if so, when? In seeking to answer these questions, I have drawn on some of the most significant UFO encounters I have come across in over thirty-five years of experience in this field. Some of them I have been connected with personally, and am responsible for bringing to public attention. However, they are included not so much for their own sake, or just because they are outstanding examples of UFO activity, but for what they tell us about those who control and man these spacecraft, and about their message for our world.

Also included is a look at the only regular series of contacts with these beings in modern times that I know for sure to be true. That is not to say they are the only genuine contacts, but no others have been proved to me personally. They are the experiences of someone I was privileged to work with for over twenty years, and see at very close quarters for much of that period, Dr George King. As a result of this, I am in a position to know that he was everything he claimed to be, and invite you to form your own conclusions.

From his earliest contacts in the 1950s, Dr King channeled what I believe to be some of the greatest teaching and most profound revelations our world has ever received, some of which are included in the final chapter of this book. I am particularly grateful to the international directors of The Aetherius Society for giving me permission to release material received from cosmic sources by Dr King, some of which has never been available in published form before. As someone who reveres the ancient wisdom—particularly from the yoga tradition—with a passion, for me the cosmic wisdom delivered through Dr King surpasses even this, and that really is saying something.

Aside from teaching, some of the early communications focused on specific, contentious issues of the time. One of these, naturally, was the worldwide cover-up of information about UFOs, which has since been well and truly exposed for the lying machine that it was, as is detailed in Chapter 3. Another was the insane march toward nuclear proliferation exacerbated by a cold war, and a third was how to prevent a third world war, which would wreak such global destruction that the Earth would take generations to recover from it. Even more significant was the program of spiritual intervention they instigated through advanced technological manipulations using extraterrestrial spacecraft and vast life-saving energies directed to our planet and its inhabitants. I will outline how some of these were accomplished, and how they are continuing to be performed to this very day.

Subjective, as well as objective, experience is of vital importance as a means of determining the truth. Some people will accept objective evidence only, and they will find that here, but in the final analysis, we often accept what we know at an intuitive level just as much, if not more, than something that has been demonstrated to us through rational deduction and intellectual argument. The big decisions we take in our personal lives are a result of our innermost feelings— we don't choose our life partner because we have been convinced to do so in a debating forum but because we know that we love them.

Reason and intuition are both valid, but intuition, if we are able to recognize it, will never let us down. Reason, on the other hand, is limited by the facts it has at its disposal. For example, based on the facts available to him, Aristotle, surely one of the fathers of logical deduction, had very little understanding of the true nature of the universe. On the other hand, at the same time, the prevalent belief in the East, based primarily on mystical and spiritual traditions, was that the universe was populated by beings inhabiting heavenly spheres, which are referred to in Buddhist writings as "lokas." Of the two, the eastern belief, which resulted from the meditations and deep intuitive realizations of enlightened teachers, was much nearer to the mark than the logical deductions of most of the ancient Greek thinkers. Aristarchus of Samos was a notable exception —he championed the heliocentric thesis—but he was a maverick in the climate of those days. The current belief in a multidimensional universe of populated planets is not a million miles from the ancient eastern idea of lokas inhabited by celestial beings, as I will explore.

Even the medieval Christian idea that the planets were inhabited by angels, based on religious theories that some would regard as nothing more than superstition, is surely closer to the truth than orthodox scientific opinion of the late twentieth century that tended toward the view that there is little or no extraterrestrial life whatsoever. I believe that spirituality and science are both routes to the truth. This admittedly conflicts with the ideas of some diehard atheistic scientists today who declare the notion of God to be a delusion and yet betray their own cherished method-ologies in doing so. It doesn't get much less scientific than to say unequivocally that God doesn't exist—something they will never be able to prove. Some of the greatest scientists in history held strong religious or spiritual beliefs—Darwin and Einstein to name just two. Others have found their belief in spiritual principles enhanced through their scientific studies—Sir Oliver Lodge and Erwin Schrœdinger are examples of this.

One of the greatest scientists who ever lived stands out as a champion of the amalgamation of science and spirituality, as well as logic and intuition—the seventeenth-century genius Sir Isaac Newton. Many people don't realize that he spent far more time researching the mystical practice of alchemy than he did any other branch of science. Some would, in my view wrongly, dismiss alchemy as so much twaddle, but it may have been his abiding interest in the mystical, as well as the physical, that enabled him to develop extraordinary perception. Insights can come to all of us under the strangest of conditions. For Newton, it was looking out of the window of Woolsthorpe Manor, his home near the English market town of Grantham, and observing an apple as it fell from a tree in the garden. Who could have guessed that, through this one seemingly haphazard event, science was about to be changed forever? How does such an apparently small epiphany as this lead to such a gigantic consequence as the discovery of gravity?

Two thousand years before Newton's apple, Archimedes discovered the principle of displacement while having a bath. He had visited the public baths countless times before, but on this occasion, at the right moment under the right conditions, the answer he was seeking came in a flash. The story goes that he ran out of the baths and down the streets of Syracuse, shouting "Eureka," the ancient Greek for "I have discovered it!"

We don't all have "eureka moments," but most of us have at least one event in our past that changed our life forever. It happened to me in Hull, in the northeast of England, where I was at university studying drama and music in the early seventies. Like most students, we had very little money and I shared a modest house with my lifelong friend, John Holder. We shared something more important as well—a deep interest in spirituality in general and The Aetherius Society in particular. UFOs were at the forefront of our interest. We believed, and still do, that they have been with us for thousands of years and that they have made specialized contacts through the ages.

John and I were keen squash players. We played it with such vehement enthusiasm that gym shoes all too often needed to be replaced. One day, I had a simple choice to make—continue to investigate the cosmic plan for our world by purchasing some more Aetherius Society teachings, or play squash in worn-out gym shoes. I chose the former. I must admit that deciding not to buy a decent pair of gym shoes does not rank among the great sacrifices of history, but it was still a choice that had to be made, and it was important to me at the time.

A few days later, hundreds of people in Hull witnessed a cigar-shaped UFO moving very slowly across the early evening sky. John and I, hearing this on the news, jumped into our battered old car and drove to the area where the UFO was reported as being seen. Sure enough, there it was, in the sky above us—a large, oblong, bright white shape. We parked the car and ran across a field to get a better view. The field was damp, from earlier rain or dew. We stood near a large oak tree in the field, watching what we were sure was a UFO. Gradually, it became obscured from our vision by the tree. I looked down, and there, beneath the tree, was a brand new pair of gym shoes, my size. I picked them up, by which time the UFO was visible again, and we watched it until it disappeared from view. Of course, I don't believe that the UFO had left the shoes there for me to find, but I do believe in synchronicity and the careful interpretation of signs. I saw it as a sign about the overriding importance of the extraterrestrial message, and if you put that first, other things you need will come to you. Since then, I have found that to be true.

This is as much a book for the spiritual seeker as it is for the UFO enthusiast. For me, there is no dichotomy between these two. Spirituality needs a cosmic dimension, and the science of the cosmos needs a spiritual dimension, as is becoming increasingly apparent. Many UFO books go out of their way to reject the spiritual approach, and few spiritual books attempt to address the significance of UFOs. So, I hope that this book will fill the void between these two and, in doing so, enhance them both.

UFO stands for "unidentified flying object" and not all UFOs are extraterrestrial spacecraft. Some can be easily identified as man-made or natural phenomena, but I have no doubt, and according to polls increasing numbers of people agree, that some are indeed vehicles from other worlds—and it takes just one sighting of an extraterrestrial spacecraft to prove that there is intelligent life elsewhere in the universe. In many ways, UFO is an unfortunate term for this phenomenon, which burst upon the scene as a source of public fascination over sixty years ago. At that time, another name was more widely used. Down-to-earth, ordinary, even banal, it caught the public imagination then and still does today. The term is flying saucer.

CHAPTER 1

The arrival of flying saucers

You can resist an invading army;
you cannot resist an idea whose time
has come.

Victor Hugo

O n June 24 1947, Kenneth Arnold, an experienced pilot, was flying a small private plane from Chehalis to Yakima in Washington State on a business trip, a journey that was of apparently little significance. He decided to make a detour en route to search for a large marine transport aircraft that had supposedly crashed near the southwest side of Mount Rainier, the most prominent peak in the Cascade Range. Failing to discover the wreckage, he made a 360-degree turn above the city of Mineral and started again toward Mount Rainier, climbing to over 9,000 feet, heading in the direction of Yakima. He enjoyed the pleasure of flying at high altitude in the smooth air, observing both sky and terrain.

He had not flown on this course for more than two or three minutes when a bright flash reflected on his airplane, startling him into thinking he may have come too close to another aircraft. But although he looked all around the sky to see where this reflection had come from, he saw nothing until he observed in the distance nine peculiar-looking craft flying from north to south, at a height of approximately 9,500 feet, in the direction of Mount Rainier. He assumed they must be jet planes, but was not able at first to make out their shape or formation. Then, as they approached the mountain, he saw their outline clearly against the snow, flying in a long line. At just one minute to 3 p.m., it was still a clear day with good visibility.

He was surprised how close these aircraft were flying to the mountaintops in the "hogback" of the mountain range. They seemed to hold a definite flight pattern while swerving between the high peaks. What bothered him as he watched their impressive display was that he could not see the aircrafts' tails, which he expected to see. He estimated that his distance from them was about twenty to twenty-five miles, and he thought that they must be quite large because he could see them so clearly. He judged their span to be as wide as the farthest engines on each side of the fuselage of a DC-4, and was upset with himself at not being able to identify exactly what type of aircraft these were.

While recounting the incident, he gave his now famous description of these UFOs as being "saucer-like." He said that the chain of nine craft was at least five miles long, and the whole sighting lasted between two and a half and three minutes. When the Sun reflected from the craft, he said, they appeared to be completely round "saucer-like disks." Although he was met with disbelief by the press, Arnold was as credible a witness as you could get. A well-educated businessman with a successful company, Great Western Fire Controls Supply, which dealt in fire suppression systems, he had more than nine thousand flying hours behind him, and had devoted considerable time to search and rescue. He was an athletic man who was, at one time, put forward to try for the US diving team. Later, he was to run, albeit unsuccessfully, for Lieutenant Governor of Idaho. This was not a "nutter."

What started out as an unremarkable business trip turned into one of the most well-known aerial journeys ever taken. Although Arnold never used the term "flying saucer"—he was using the example of the saucer-shaped disks that some people enjoy skimming across water to illustrate the flight patterns of these objects—he will go down in history as the man who coined what is now a household name for UFOs. For better or for worse, it has stuck.

To understand the significance of this event, you have to try to adopt the mindset that existed in those days. A Gallup poll commissioned in August 1947 asked the question "What do you think these saucers are?" and got the following results:

No answer/don't know:	33 percent
Imagination, optical illusions, mirages:	29 percent
Hoax:	10 percent
US secret weapon, part of atomic bomb:	15 percent
Weather forecasting devices:	3 percent
Russian secret weapon:	1 percent
Searchlights on airplanes:	2 percent
Other:	9 percent
Total (some chose more than one):	102 percent

It is amazing to think now that just 9 percent in this poll believed there could be an explanation that might include the existence of extraterrestrial craft. The possibility was clearly not considered credible enough even to specify in the poll. Just forty years later, in March 1987, Gallup commissioned another poll in which it was shown that just a third of the American public denied the existence of UFOs and extraterrestrial life—50 percent of those polled expressed the belief that there are "people somewhat like ourselves living on other planets in the universe" while 34 percent were skeptical of this assertion. The poll showed that 49 percent thought that UFOs were real with only 30 percent being doubtful.

Subsequent polls confirm the same trend. One conducted for *Newsweek* in 1996 showed that 48 percent believed in UFOs and 29 percent believed that we have made contact with alien beings. A Gallup poll conducted the following year told the same story with again 48 percent of Americans believing that UFOs are real. In the same year, a poll conducted for CNN/*Time* magazine came up with the unexpected finding that 64 percent of Americans believed that aliens have contacted humans on this Earth. Probably the most startling poll in the 1990s was conducted for a television program, shown on ITV in Britain, entitled "Strange but True"—92 percent of those viewers who voted believed that aliens are visiting this Earth. In 2002, a similar survey for Sky News in the UK showed that 65 percent of voting viewers believed in UFOs. A YouGov poll for the *Sun* newspaper in 2008 showed that 9 percent of those polled had seen a UFO and a further 43 percent believed that they existed compared with 36 percent who believed that they did not.

Many other surveys could be cited. Overall, they show an increasing tendency for people to believe in UFOs, life on other planets, and contact by aliens with people on Earth throughout history, confounding the idea that these are strange, eccentric views held by a tiny minority. It is not really surprising that there has been a sea-change in opinion about inhabited planets throughout the universe when you consider the scientific breakthroughs that have been made in recent decades. One researcher at Edinburgh University, Duncan Forgan, for example, concluded in 2009 that there could be tens of thousands of intelligent civilizations in our galaxy, and he was referring to life as we know it, very similar to our own. Forgan, whose work was reported in the *International Journal of Astrobiology*, simulated a galaxy much like our own, allowing it to develop solar systems based on what is known about our galaxy. These simulated alien worlds were subject to three different scenarios, each with different parameters for evolution. The most negative of these indicated that 361 civilizations existed in the galaxy, the second concluded that there were 31,513, and the final model produced a figure of 37,964.

Another scientific development in 2009, from a different field of research, also suggested an increasing likelihood of life as we know it occurring elsewhere in the universe. An analysis, by NASA scientists, of tiny particles captured by the Stardust comet-chasing probe revealed traces of an amino acid called glycine. This is a basic component of proteins that life as we know it requires, and this was the first time it had been discovered in space. The scientists deduced from this that life may have been carried to Earth by comets colliding with the planet. This means that other planets are likely to have been seeded with amino acids in the same way, suggesting that life may have evolved there, too. Carl Pilcher, director of the NASA Astrobiology Institute, was quoted as saying that the discovery of glycine in a comet supports the idea that the fundamental building blocks of life are prevalent in space, and strengthens the argument that life in the universe may be common rather than rare.

These are just two recent scientific developments that support the concept of extraterrestrial existence. The situation was very different in 1947 when Kenneth Arnold had his extraordinary and pivotal flying saucer experience. It was just not the done thing then to believe in something so bizarre, unconventional, and challenging to established thinking as life on other planets, or beings who could bring their spacecraft in close proximity to Earth.

The world had just emerged from the tragic and horrific conflict of World War Two, with shocking revelations of unprecedented cruelty in the infamous Nazi and Japanese concentration camps. What people craved then was stability, prosperity, and, above all, peace. Faced with the prospect of a cold war and the emergence of nuclear warfare as a very real like... people in the capitalist West wanted ordinariness and conventionality.

It seems strange now to think of a time when it was taken as read that a man would wear a jacket and tie to walk down the road to mail a letter, and when a woman wearing trousers would be seen as an affront to decency. It was also a time when most people in America and Europe would describe themselves as practicing Christians, and governments were held in high esteem. Politicians were seen as worthy men and, very occasionally, women, and none more so than the man who had maintained the morale of the world through exceptionally dangerous days, Winston Churchill.

Churchill was also the man who had presided over the first inquiry into what we would now call a UFO, when he was First Lord of the Admiralty in 1912. This concerned an object seen over Sheerness in Kent, England, which at the time was suspected of being a German Zeppelin, although subsequent inquiries ruled out that possibility. Many years later, on July 28 1952, Prime Minister Churchill asked his Air Minister, "What does all this stuff about flying saucers amount to? What can it mean? What is the truth?" If this memo tells us one thing, it is surely that even the man who should have been more in the know than anyone else in the land was uncertain about this phenomenon. Far from ruling it out, he was seeking answers.

Churchill's memo was prompted by a significant sighting of UFOs above Washington DC in the summer of 1952, during which the flying objects showed up on radar and outpaced the most advanced jet fighters of the time. The implications of this event not only impacted on the administration of the then President of the USA, Harry S. Truman, but also reached the British government. The memo was addressed to the Lord De L'Isle and Dudley, who was Secretary of State for Air. The reply Churchill received, couched in the prosaic phraseology so typical of bureaucratic correspondence, was breathtaking in its blatant skepticism. The minute from the Secretary of State gave a bland assurance to the Prime Minister that flying saucers presented no cause for concern, that all incidents could be accounted for by mistaken identity, delusions, and hoaxes, and that the Americans had reached the same conclusions.

To describe this response to the Prime Minister's request for the truth about such a vitally important subject as woefully inadequate would be to flatter it. It was signed off by Churchill's official Scientific Adviser, Lord Cherwell, with the unconvincing assertion that he agreed entirely with the Secretary of State's conclusions. If the Prime Minister was being fobbed off by half truths, what chance did the public have? A previous Chief Scientific Adviser, Sir Henry Tizard, had set up a small working party to investigate the flying saucer phenomenon and, according to minutes, had felt that "reports of flying saucers ought not to be dismissed without some investigation." The findings of this working party are now regarded by some researchers as incomplete to say the least, and yet it was based on the results of these findings that Churchill had received his dismissive response.

Incidentally, this working party had been dissolved the previous year and it's possible that personal politics may have had some influence in the matter. Lord Cherwell was a long time rival of Sir Henry Tizard, who had been the great enthusiast in the Ministry of Defence for seriously investigating the flying saucer phenomenon. If it really does come down to petty point-scoring between two men in a government office, can we wonder at the fact that the controllers of flying saucers have not yet decided to engage openly in discussions with political leaders from this planet?

Political machinations aside, cultural conditioning at the time flew in the face of flying saucers. The existence of alien beings visiting our world in advanced spacecraft, demonstrating a technology light years ahead of our own, just did not fit with the desires and inclinations of people who wanted security through the familiar certainties of life. Debunking and ridicule of a challenging discovery chimed in well with the aspirations of many in that period, but not of all. It was also a time of unprecedented cultural change in the music and fashion of the young, and a period when opportunity was starting to be extended to the less privileged in society.

Some say that the art of a conman is based on the fact that the victim of his con is complicit in the exercise. The theory goes that the person being conned wishes at some level to be so deceived, chooses to be gullible, accepts the process, knowing somewhere in the deep recesses of his or her mind that it is taking place. If this is true, then arguably the media and official spokesmen were providing what much of the public wanted—a convenient way to dismiss a truth that was staring them in the eyes. To the serious, open-minded investigator, there could be no doubt that the flying saucer had arrived. The explanations and what we now know to be lies put out by officialdom may have been music to the ears of those who did not want to believe in the possible existence of extraterrestrial visitors.

Even during World War Two, there were incidents too explicit to ignore. Strange balls of light and small, metallic objects were sighted by allied and British pilots flying missions over wartime Europe. The US Air Force called these objects "Foo Fighters." The word "Foo" was taken from "Smokey Stover," a cartoon strip by Bill Holman, which was much loved by radar operator Donald J. Meiers, who first coined the term. US night-fighter pilots based in France revealed how strange balls of fire had been following their planes over Germany. These mysterious objects appeared to follow them at high speeds for miles, and were often seen to zoom upward into the sky. Some pilots described them as being like Christmas tree lights. In a classic piece of debunking, some scientists tried to explain away these sightings as the after-images of dazzle caused by flak bursts. What an insult to the highly trained pilots who had observed them and made factual reports of what they had seen!

The next big event to trigger a seismic change in attitudes to our extraterrestrial visitors, and a subject of fascination to this day, was an extraordinary occurrence at Roswell. Just a matter of days after Kenneth Arnold's historic flight over Mount Rainier, stories started to emerge of a crashed UFO on a ranch approximately 75 miles northwest of Roswell in New Mexico. The event was reported to the authorities by the rancher, William "Mack" Brazel, on July 6. On July 8, the Roswell Army Air Field (RAAF) formally announced in a press release that it had recovered a "flying disk." On the same day, the local newspaper, *Roswell Daily Record*, reported on its front page that the Roswell Army Air Field had come into possession of a flying saucer. No details of its construction or appearance, the paper reported, had yet been revealed. It did describe, though, the sighting by two local residents, Mr and Mrs Dan Wilmot, of what appeared to be an oval-shaped object, like two inverted saucers facing each other, traveling at between four and five hundred miles per hour approximately 1,500 feet above them. They said it glowed as though lights were shining from the inside. Wilmot, who is described in the article as one of the most respected and reliable citizens in town, estimated, according to the newspaper, that it was fifteen to twenty feet in diameter. The following day, the same newspaper reported that the "flying disk" was in fact a weather balloon or some other weather device.

Brazel had discovered debris, which he believed may have been part of a flying saucer, scattered widely over his ranch. He reported this to the local sheriff in Roswell, George Wilcox, who informed the local US Air Force base. Officers from the base retrieved some of the debris, which was later flown to research laboratories in Ohio. Later it was claimed that the UFO itself was recovered and flown to a more prominent site. This incident was backed up by UFO sightings reported during the same week by local residents. It could be seen as a small, localized prototype for the disinformation that was to follow internationally through the media and from government sources. The cover-up mechanism went into action and US Army Air officials stated that it was definitely not a UFO but a weather balloon. It has been a focus for ufologists, researchers, and conspiracy theorists generally ever since.

Opinions range from complete disbelief in the whole event through to the idea that it was a crashed UFO containing aliens who were captured by the American government. Personally, I would dismiss both these interpretations as too extreme. Undoubtedly, something happened. Local ranchers in New Mexico had nothing to gain, particularly in the climate of those days, from inventing such a yarn, and even if they had, their claims would not have been supported, as they were at first so emphatically, by the Roswell Army Air Field. On the other hand, it is difficult to believe that alien beings who could traverse the skies of the cosmos and get this close to our planet would be so incompetent as to first crash and then be captured by a civilization that, to them, might be as primitive as a colony of insects would be to us.

The incident at Roswell has become an icon in ufology, so much so that in 1997, on the fiftieth anniversary of its occurrence, some hundred thousand pilgrims made their way to this spot to commemorate the event. A television series, known variously as "Roswell" and "Roswell High," which was made between 1999 and 2002 in the USA, is still broadcast in various parts of the world, including the UK. It draws on the Roswell incident as a basis for its science-fiction theme.

To this day, the public have not seen any definite hardware, i.e. the "nuts and bolts" of a real flying saucer. One theory is that it is in a military base somewhere, another is that it is being used for reverse engineering, but both are just theories. Attempts to use the Freedom of Information Act to obtain Roswell UFO-related documents from agencies, such as the CIA, have been repeatedly stonewalled. Claims are made that the documents either don't exist or cannot be released for security reasons.

If a UFO did crash at Roswell in the first week of July 1947, my first inclination would be to believe that it had done so deliberately in order to stimulate interest in the phenomenon. It is very unlikely that any aliens would have died—and I would discount the possibility of any allowing themselves to be captured by the American Air Force and dying in captivity, as some have claimed. They may, however, have used this incident in some way to start a process of revelation about the nature of their craft. If so, the opportunity was not taken up by the authorities as it should have been. Instead, a policy of disinformation kicked in to action. Ufologists have not always covered themselves in glory, either, over this incident, most notably when a film claiming to be the autopsy of an alien captured at Roswell was produced in 1995 and, after being believed by some, was exposed as a hoax.

Today, the Roswell incident has become part of the local tourist industry. The International UFO Museum and Research Center in Roswell was incorporated as a nonprofit-making organization in 1991 and opened to the public in 1992. Its co-founder was former Roswell Army Air Field public information officer Lt Walter Haut, who had issued the original press release to the local media in 1947 under the direction, he claimed, of the local base commander. The museum is said to contain some alleged debris and evidence of the incident. Whatever your view, the Roswell incident is certainly forever enshrined in UFO lore. What we know of it could accurately be described, to paraphrase Churchill's description of Russia in 1939, as a riddle, wrapped in a mystery, inside an enigma.

The sensationalism around flying saucers in the press was as nothing compared with the mythology being created in Hollywood. The occasional science-fiction film had been produced in both America and Europe since the beginning of the twentieth century, and the legendary radio adaptation of H.G. Wells's novel *The War of the Worlds*, directed and narrated by Orson Welles, went out on the Columbia Broadcasting System Radio Network on October 30 1938, on their Halloween program. The story, which was centered around a Martian invasion, was broadcast as though it was real news, and caused panic among some listeners. The debate still continues about just how much panic there was, and whether large numbers were really planning, as was reported, to vacate their homes and set off in the hope of finding somewhere safer to hide from the invasion. At the very least, there was widespread outrage about the confusion caused, which also shows how much potential belief in alien life existed.

From the 1950s, the science-fiction genre really came into its own—in quantity if not always in quality, considering that many of these films were low-budget "B" movies. With the notable exception of "The Day the Earth Stood Still" (1951), most emphasized the supposed horrific aspects of the phenomenon, with such titles as "The Thing from Another World" (1951), "Radar Men from the Moon" (1952), "Invaders from Mars" (1953), and "It came from Outer Space" (1953). More recently, there have been film remakes of some of the most effective of these, with "The War of the Worlds" reappearing in 2005 starring Tom Cruise, and "The Day the Earth Stood Still" in 2008 starring Keanu Reeves.

It's not unknown for soap-opera fans to try to emulate the behavior and language of their favorite characters in their own lives, whether consciously or unconsciously. In a similar way, science fiction subtly infiltrated people's approach to what was a brand new phenomenon, the flying saucer. The horror motif started to infect the attitudes of some of those who did believe in extraterrestrial spacecraft and our alien visitors, egged on by the vivid, far-fetched depictions of the film industry. For a fictional work to be successful, the viewer, listener, or reader has to be able to believe it is possible. In some cases, this demands a major suspension of disbelief on their part, but without it they could not really get into the storyline and take it seriously enough to be engaged by it. The fact that the burgeoning science-fiction industry from the 1950s up to the present day has been such a major part of our culture, also shows that people are sufficiently open to the reality of the existence of extraterrestrial spacecraft and contacts with their inhabitants to buy into their portrayal in the movies.

Perhaps it was the skepticism of various governments that motivated those who wanted to believe in this phenomenon to turn to the science-fiction arena. The official approach was stultifying in its dismissal of the whole notion of flying saucers while surreptitiously investigating their significance. The first investigation, named Project Saucer, was initiated by the US Air Force in 1947, following Kenneth Arnold's sighting. On January 22 1948, this was officially recognized and renamed Project Sign. In February 1949, it became Project Grudge, which, based on the name, seems a candid admission of how the authorities truly felt about the whole process. On September 11 1951, Captain Edward James Ruppelt took over the investigation and in 1952 it was renamed Project Blue Book. It was Captain Ruppelt, a US Air Force officer, who introduced the acronym UFO (unidentified flying object) to replace flying saucer. For all the unimaginative mundaneness of using a moving piece of crockery to describe an extraterrestrial spacecraft, it had one big advantage over UFO. It had, at least, come to represent an otherworldly vehicle, whereas UFO, to some people, could mean just about anything.

In 1953, the CIA sponsored a meeting with Air Force UFO project personnel, which they called the Robertson Panel, after the man who led it, Dr H.P. Robertson, a physicist from the California Institute of Technology (Caltech). It was not until 1974, when a document from the Robertson Panel meeting, originally classified as secret, was released under the Freedom of Information Act, that the CIA was shown to have specifically recommended adopting a policy of debunking UFOs.

In the meantime, serious, nonfiction UFO books were starting to appear. Perhaps the most influential of these was *The Flying Saucers are Real* by Major Donald Keyhoe of the US Marine Air Corps, which was published in 1950. In this, and in other articles and books, he claimed to disclose information gleaned from Air Force intelligence reports he had been given by his contacts within the Air Force. In one television interview on CBS in January 1958, on a show called "The Armstrong Circle Theater," Major Keyhoe was actually cut off in mid-sentence by the producers when he attempted to expose the truth about the government's interest in UFOs. It later emerged that he had wanted to reveal that a 1948 top-secret report had concluded UFOs were interplanetary, and that in 1952 an intelligence analysis went even further in concluding they were intelligently maneuvered.

A groundbreaking article appeared on April 7 1952 in *Life* magazine, entitled "Have we visitors from space?" Printed on the cover of this magazine, alongside a classic shot of Hollywood legend Marilyn Monroe, is the statement: "There is a case for interplanetary saucers." The authors of the article, H.B. Darrach Jr and Robert Ginna, attested that the Air Force was ready to concede that many sightings defied explanation, and they proceeded to offer what they saw as scientific evidence for these craft. Among their claims were the facts that the Air Force was maintaining an ongoing intelligence investigation and study of unidentified aerial objects; military aircraft were being alerted to attempt interception; and radar and photographic equipment was available to obtain further data about them. The authors also suggested that the Air Force hoped to recover actual unidentified objects, if possible. Based on this article, you might conclude that high-ranking generals in the Pentagon took the notion that we do indeed have visitors from space very seriously. However, just months later, the Air Force were engaged in attempting to explain away credible sightings as weather phenomena.

In the 1960s, it was more of the same. Occasionally, a crack appeared in the fabricated wall of silence, such as when astronaut James McDivitt of Gemini 4 admitted on October 5 1965 at a press conference in Dallas, Texas, that there was no doubt that UFOs existed. Later in the same year, two other astronauts, Frank Borman and James A. Lovell, in spacecraft Gemini 7, reported the sighting of a UFO. A significant admission was made by Dr James E. MacDonald, a leading atmospheric physicist, on August 7 1968 during a talk to the Boeing Management Association. He noted that extraterrestrial visitors could be multidimensional and have a psychic or spiritual significance. Meanwhile, in the Soviet Union, an article by Russian scientist Dr Felix Ziegel appeared in the magazine *Soviet Life* in February 1967, confirming that UFOs were being sighted in the Soviet Union, and stating that their extraterrestrial origin should be seriously considered.

However, these hopeful signs of honesty and openness were soon counterbalanced by the dead hand of officialdom. In January 1969, the National Academy of Sciences approved the Condon Report, which was to bring inertia to even the halfhearted gestures that occasionally emerged from the body politic. The struggle to breathe life into the truth of this phenomenon was served a serious blow by this report, which was named after Dr Edward Condon of the University of Colorado, a figure who is regarded with deep suspicion by many ufologists. It was to bring an end to Project Blue Book, which you could be forgiven for regarding as fairly inconsequential anyway, given its relative impotence, but which at least had provided some small semblance of a quest for the truth.

At over nine hundred pages, the report is a weighty document. I have not read it myself but it is regarded as being full of inbuilt contradictions. For example, it mentions that over 30 percent of the UFO sightings analyzed could not be explained by the scientists who investigated them yet concludes there is nothing to be gained from further research into the subject. And if you believe that, you'll believe anything! Even more regrettably, the report was taken seriously by many in the media at the time, including journals such as *Science*.

Entitled "Scientific Study of Unidentified Flying Objects" it could have been more aptly named "A Roadblock to the Truth," but although the blow delivered to revealing the truth about UFOs was serious, it was not fatal. Some lone voices, such as Dr MacDonald's, continued to present a dissenting view. Dr J. Allen Hynek, who was consultant to the Air Force on UFOs, described the report as a strange sort of scientific paper that did not fulfill the promise of its title. He said that it left the same odd, inexplicable residue of unsolved cases that had plagued the US Air Force investigation for twenty years. Yet despite this, the Air Force accepted the recommendations of the Condon Report and officially closed down Project Blue Book and their research into UFOs.

As he set out to sail around the world, Sir Francis Drake wrote to Sir Francis Walsingham, a prominent statesman of the time, "Continuing on to the end, until it be thoroughly finished, yields the only true glory." Thankfully, the dispiriting and inglorious act of government obfuscation in officially abandoning UFO research was far from the end of the flying saucer/UFO phenomenon. The search continued, both behind the scenes at government level and among the increasingly fascinated public, to find what the arrival of these objects in our skies really meant. To understand that, you need to turn to the people who were directly contacted by those who manned them.

CHAPTER 2

They make contact

Some are born great, some achieve greatness, and some have greatness thrust upon them.

William Shakespeare

As the renowned underwater explorer Jacques Cousteau said, when a man has the opportunity to lead an extraordinary life, he has no right to keep it to himself. This could not be more appropriately applied than to those who have been contacted by extraterrestrials. UFO contactees fall into three categories: fake, deluded, and genuine. Of these three, the last one is, in my view, the least common. The category definitely exists, though—I wouldn't be writing this book at all if it didn't. As for the other two categories, I would estimate that there are more deluded claims than fake ones nowadays, although it may have been different in the late 1940s and early 1950s. At that time, conmen and hoaxers may well have thought a claim to be in touch with beings from other worlds was a marketable prospect. For the most part this has not proved to be the case. On the contrary, the main response has been ridicule and verbal abuse with, on the whole, very little financial remuneration.

The deluded category is more complex. Obviously, there are those who might be described as mentally challenged, who genuinely believe certain events are occurring, which are not, and who are unable to tell the difference between a vivid imagination and reality. Others have had genuine experiences of one kind or another that they have wrongly interpreted as alien contact. Such people are not lying, because they believe what they say, but they are not really in touch with beings from other worlds. They may be in touch with astral entities from this world, or some other paranormal incident that is very much of this Earth may have occurred in their life. In some cases they may have met someone whom they wrongly believe to be extraterrestrial. Careful discrimination and proper investigation are the best ways to determine how substantial their claims— abduction is the most common—really are.

I prefer to focus on claims that are, or could be, genuine and, although far from an exhaustive survey, those that follow include some of the most significant ones. The contact that I consider to be the most important of this era was made with Dr George King. Before that, however, came the experience of the most famous contactee of modern times, Polish-born American George Adamski (1891–1965). On October 9 1946 he was in the yard of his home in Palomar Gardens, California, with some companions, watching a meteor shower. Many others in the region were doing the same thing that night. Adamski and his friends had been about to go indoors after the most intense part of the meteor shower had finished when he, and others with him, noticed a large, black object in the sky, hovering above the mountain ridge to the south of Mount Palomar toward San Diego. He described it as being similar in shape to a gigantic airship, but it was not moving. His first thought was that this could be some new type of aircraft developed during the war, which was being used by scientists to collect data on the falling meteors at high altitude. But as the group continued to watch, the craft pointed upward and shot into space, leaving a fiery trail behind it that lingered for at least five minutes.

When they did return to the house, they heard a radio report on a San Diego station announcing that a large cigar-shaped spaceship had hovered over the city and was witnessed by hundreds of people. This, they realized, must be the same object that they had just seen. Adamski said that his first instinct was to try to explain away the sighting on the basis that interplanetary travel was impossible, but six military officers, whom he later met in a café in San Diego, informed him that the spaceship was not of this Earth. Adamski was an amateur astronomer. He had two telescopes, to one of which he could attach a camera, which he used for celestial photography. After this experience, he decided to observe the skies more closely than ever. Sky watching was already his hobby—it now became his obsession.

One Friday evening in the summer of 1947, he was sitting alone, watching the sky, as had become his wont, when he noticed a bright, illuminated object moving from east to west above the mountain ridge. This was followed by others. One of these objects stopped in mid-space and reversed its path of travel. By then the Kenneth Arnold sighting was well known and Adamski concluded he must be watching a flying saucer. He called four people from inside the house to come out and observe the incredible spectacle—he said 184 objects were passing in single file, mainly in squadrons of thirty-two. Some of the objects disappeared to the west, while others turned toward the south, and the observers noticed that they appeared to have a ring around a central body or dome. The last one hovered for several seconds, shooting out two powerful beams of light, one toward the south, the other north. Other people in the vicinity also witnessed this extraordinary, multiple flying saucer visitation.

Late in 1949, Adamski says he was approached by four military officers to request his cooperation in trying to photograph UFOs in space, because of the versatility of his equipment. They were apparently approaching others in the region as well. Shortly after this, he did indeed manage to get two interesting photographs, which he passed to the military officers concerned, only to receive a complete denial of their legitimacy from the Air Force. He resolved to continue in earnest but not to hand over any of his photographs to these officers. He stayed out, come rain or shine, watching the heavens and hoping to get an indisputable photograph of a flying saucer. He took many photographs during this period, but still did not have the spectacular shot he was looking for. One of the photographs, taken on May 29 1950, was to be depicted years later on an August 1978 commemorative stamp issued by Grenada in order to mark what that country had designated the "Year of UFOs." Grenada's then Prime Minister, Sir Eric Gairy, was a firm believer in the existence of extraterrestrial spacecraft and wished to encourage other world leaders at the United Nations to engage in active UFO research.

Adamski's connection with flying saucers was soon to surpass photography. He claimed that, shortly after twelve noon on Thursday, November 20 1952, he made personal contact with a being from another world. It happened in the California desert just over ten miles from Desert Center toward Parker, Arizona. He had made many unfruitful visits to various locations, following information about flying saucer sightings. This time he had been told of sightings in the desert by some people who lived locally, and six others accompanied him to the spot. He says that, suddenly and simultaneously, they all looked around and saw, high above them, a completely soundless and gigantic, cigar-shaped silver spacecraft without wings or any appendages. It came in their direction and hovered, but was gone before any photographs could be taken.

Adamski felt that contact could be made. He took his telescope and camera and separated from the group, remaining in their sight but leaving them to observe the sky from nearby. Suddenly, he saw a flash in the sky and a small craft appearing to drift between the mountain peaks about half a mile away from him. Quickly, he started to take photographs, and then saw a man standing at the entrance of a ravine between two hills, beckoning to him. He wondered if it was a prospector, although no one had passed them on the road. Could he really be someone who lived in these mountains? Adamski walked toward him, all the while in full view of his companions. As he approached, he noticed that the man seemed to be wearing trousers that Adamski described as being like ski trousers. He was particularly surprised by this, because he would not have expected to find anyone wearing such trousers in a desert. The man had long, sandy-colored hair reaching to his shoulders – an extremely unusual sight in those days, although Adamski had seen men wearing their hair almost that long before. The man looked young and smiled at him, but it wasn't until Adamski came close to him that he knew he was in the presence of a being from another world. So beautiful was he, with such a pleasing visage, that Adamski lost all thought for himself. He felt like a child in the presence of one of great wisdom and love, who radiated a feeling of kindness, understanding, and complete humility.

This alien being extended his hand, not to shake Adamski's as he expected, but to place it palm-to-palm with Adamski's, not too firmly, as a gesture of friendship. The texture of the skin was delicate, firm, and warm. The hand was slender with long fingers. Adamski estimated him to be five foot six inches tall and around 135lb in weight. His age was difficult to determine, but he could have been taken for a twenty-eight year old. He was round-faced with a high forehead, large, serene, gray-green eyes, a fine nose, and an average-sized mouth. He seemed to have a medium suntan and a smooth, unbearded complexion. His one-piece, brown garment, possibly some kind of uniform, had a high collar, long sleeves, and bands around the wrists. He also had a band around his waist, and the weave of the garment was different from any material Adamski could identify, appearing to give off a sheen. It had no zippers, buttons, buckles, fasteners, or pockets. The man's shoes were also of a woven material, which looked like leather, and seemed to be soft and flexible.

Adamski attempted to talk to him, but the extraterrestrial shook his head. Adamski was familiar with the concept of telepathy from his metaphysical and philosophical studies, so he tried to use this as a method of communication, combined with hand gestures. From this, he learned that the visitors were from Venus, that they were friendly, and that one of their main concerns was the atomic experimentation now being undertaken on Earth. The communication continued, leading in a more spiritual direction, including the existence of God and the universal laws of creation, which, he was told, they, unlike the people of Earth, followed exactly. Eventually, Adamski returned to his companions, who had seen the small craft but not the visitor, although they did see his footprints, which were embedded in the ground. Photographs were allegedly taken of them, and sketches made. Plaster of Paris casts of one of the footprints were also taken.

As a significant footnote to this incident, just over three weeks later, on December 13 1952, from his property in Palomar Gardens, George Adamski took some photographs of a flying saucer, a return visit that he said had been promised by the alien being. Of these, three turned out to be good in detail and they go down as among the most significant flying saucer photographs in history. Portholes, spherical landing gear, and a light on top of the cabin show clearly. The craft was made of a translucent metal and was about thirty-five feet in diameter with a white line around the base of the dome, seeming to be some form of power coil, according to Adamski. Before the flying saucer departed, an object was dropped from it—a photographic plate

Adamski said he had given the visitor in the desert. On it, he claimed, was a symbolic photograph and image, which has never yet been fully deciphered.

A full account of this pivotal close encounter is described in a classic book published in 1953, *Flying Saucers Have Landed* by Desmond Leslie and George Adamski. Although it is now out of print, secondhand copies occasionally become available. Leslie also claimed to see UFOs, specifically in the company of Adamski while visiting him in California, and was well versed in mystical teachings, especially those of theosophy.

It is not hard to guess what kind of public reaction George Adamski received to his claims, both then and throughout his life until he died in Washington on April 23 1965, despite the fact that all six of his companions were said to have signed a sworn affidavit, confirming what they witnessed. This was not helped by the fact that later Adamski spoke of further contacts and even rides inside flying saucers. He was in demand on the lecture and media circuit, and it is claimed that he had a private audience with Queen Juliana of the Netherlands in 1959, and one with Pope John XXIII in 1963 just before the Pope's death that year. Numerous attempts have been made to debunk the photographs taken, but some of these efforts have themselves been proven to be false. For example, the chairman of a major UFO society in Britain in the 1970s claimed the pictures were of a beer cooler, until he discovered that the beer cooler in question was invented and manufactured after the photographs were taken. Adamski's subsequent claims undermine his credibility for many people, even in the UFO movement, but the story of his original contact in the desert does accord with other claims made during that period and since then, and I, for one, can fully believe it. Perhaps it was all part of a gradual extraterrestrial plan of subtle revelation, not just to government institutions, but to ordinary people.

George Adamski was not the first in America to claim direct contact with an alien being in the modern era. On Independence Day, July 4 1949 or 1950 (different accounts vary on the year), Dan Fry, a technician who worked at the Aerojet General Corporation at White Sands Proving Grounds—a large military installation in New Mexico—witnessed an episode that later became known as the White Sands Incident. Apparently, he had intended to go to Las Cruces to join the celebrations and see the firework display, but missed the last bus into town, so he found himself stranded in the almost empty army camp.

At about 8.30 p.m. he decided to go for a walk, since it was cooler outside than in, and strolled toward the base of the Organ Mountains under a bright moonlit sky. As he was looking up, one of the stars seemed to disappear. This was followed by another one, and then two more until an object, which had been obscuring these stars from his sight, came into view. He described how he felt an odd sensation traveling up his spine as the object came toward him, and his first instinct was to run away, but he realized that would be foolish. As it came closer, he could see that it was traveling at no more than fifteen to twenty miles per hour, and slowing down. He said that he watched it glide in gently and land without any bump about seventy feet away from him. The only sound was the crackling of brush beneath it as it landed. This was at the height of the cold war and Fry, who worked in rocket and missile development, thought to himself, if the Russians have a ship like this, God help America! But after one look at it, he knew that no one on Earth would be capable of developing such a vehicle. Fry approached the craft, circling around it, his curiosity overcoming any thoughts of fear. He described it as a spheroid, flattened at the top and bottom, about sixteen feet high and thirty feet at the widest point, which was about seven feet from the ground. The surface was like polished metal, silver in color with a slight violet iridescence. He said it was more like a soup bowl inverted over a sauce dish than saucer-shaped. Crockery seems to have been the terminology of choice in some of the early UFO encounters!

Fry was aware of the ridicule he was likely to attract if he spoke of this encounter. For this reason, and also because it would take some time to get back to base, he did not immediately rush off to report the incident. He touched the metal surface, finding it a few degrees above air temperature and incredibly smooth, like the surface of a large pearl. His fingertips tingled and he heard a crisp voice, which seemed to come out of the air, warning him, in English, not to touch. According to Fry, the use by this voice of American lingo, such as "pal" and "buddy," helped to remove any feeling of fear. During the ensuing conversation, Fry was informed that the visitors were attempting to determine how adaptable human beings could be to concepts foreign to their mode of thought. In short, they wanted to know whether the human mind had advanced sufficiently to be receptive to help from an extraterrestrial source, which, he was told, had not been the case in the past. The communicator, who was using what appeared to Fry to be a speaker or some form of audio system, was impressed that Fry's curiosity had overcome his fear. What they were looking for, apparently, were minds sufficiently open to receive evidence that contradicted current terrestrial thinking.

The communicator expounded some philosophical thoughts, telling Fry that he had not been picked at random and inviting him to enter the spacecraft, which his host described as being a remote-controlled cargo carrier. The speaker was not in the craft but in a mother ship nine hundred miles away. An oval-shaped opening appeared about five feet in height and three feet wide to the left of Fry and he went in, finding himself in a small passenger compartment about nine feet long, seven feet wide, and six feet high. A moving-picture projector on the wall had no visible film spools or other moving parts. He was invited to choose one of the seats, and was then taken on the journey of a lifetime—to New York and back in about thirty minutes, which Fry estimated to have entailed a speed of some eight thousand miles per hour. Along the way he was given scientific and philosophical information as well as encouragement to develop greater telepathic communication. He was also informed about previous civilizations on Earth, Atlantis and Mu or Lemuria.

I came across Dan Fry some thirty years ago at a meeting of his organization, Understanding Inc., when he was elderly but still adamant about the authenticity of his claims. In our brief conversation, I found him to be unassuming, down-to-earth, and perfectly credible. However, that was not the general view of him at the time. The deliberately skewed public perception of the White Sands Incident has been one of cynicism, ridicule, and disbelief, but none of that makes it untrue. It is a very significant account, which conforms in content to other credible accounts.

The other American contactee I would single out from that period is a man I knew fairly well, the late Dr Frank Stranges. He became a close friend of Dr King, and was a member of The Aetherius Society, as well as running his own organizations, International Evangelism Crusades Inc. and the International Theological Seminary, in Van Nuys, California. He also founded the National Investigations Committee on UFOs. He was most unusual in combining a fervent Christian evangelical faith with a firm belief in UFOs and his own claimed contact with an alien being. Having spoken alongside him at conventions and other events in the USA, I can vouch for his stirring rhetoric, comprehensive knowledge, particularly of biblical accounts of UFOs, and distinctive sense of humor, again often biblically related. He could attract thousands to his rousing speeches on evangelical themes, as he did when he visited South Korea, for example. At the same time, he was a brave champion of the authenticity of UFO contacts and their connection with spirituality. Serious consideration should, in my view, be given to all his evidence, although, as ever, it is for the reader to decide.

Dr Stranges claimed that on March 16 1957, in Alexandria, Virginia, a being from the planet Venus landed his craft and was confronted by two police officers with their weapons drawn. A government official, Harley Andrew Byrd, who worked for the Chief of Naval Information in the security clearance section for Project Blue Book, said he received an urgent message in mid March 1957 from the Alexandria Police Department, to say that two on-duty police officers had picked up an alien in human form. This alien was taken in the officers' patrol car to Washington DC to meet with the Under Secretary of Defense at the Pentagon, and later with President Eisenhower himself, accompanied by Vice President Richard Nixon. According to Byrd, this meeting lasted for nearly an hour, after which the alien was put on VIP status under the given name of Valiant Thor.

According to Dr Stranges's account, an advocate of the UFO/alien situation within the Pentagon, named as Nancy Warren, decided to contact him because he was a minister and a private investigator. Dr Stranges was in Washington for two weeks at the time, as a guest speaker at the National Evangelistic Center. He was introduced to Valiant Thor who, he said, had come to warn the President of the precarious situation in the world, particularly in relation to the arms race —a theme that dominates many of the claimed contacts during the forties, fifties, and sixties. Valiant Thor allegedly stayed on Earth for three years before returning to his own planet, Venus. He endorsed, according to Dr Stranges, the continued teachings of Jesus Christ, whom he said was a great presence in the universe, and predicted that a new era of knowledge, wisdom, and understanding would come to our planet. I know this case could sound like a conspiracy theory of almost absurd proportions, but that of itself does not make it untrue. What is of particular interest to me is, once again, the endorsement of spiritual teachings given by this alien visitor, albeit those to which Dr Stranges was already committed. Had he met with a Buddhist monk, perhaps the endorsement would have been given to that great spiritual philosophy.

So far all these contacts have taken place in the USA, but accounts of alien contacts with prominent officials were not confined to America. At least one high-placed British official in the 1950s had an experience of direct contact with what he believed could have been an alien being. The late Sir Peter Horsley was a member of the Royal Household who later became an Air Marshal and was knighted for his services. Only in later life was he willing to disclose his secret encounter, which he did in his memoirs, *Sounds From Another Room*. I was able to speak with him about it on the telephone just before the book was published. He was abroad at the time. As a result of this conversation I was among the first to reveal the full story of Sir Peter's extraordinary encounter with an alien being. It appeared on the front page of the *Sun* on August 26 1997 and in several other newspapers. What I find of particular interest is not so much the physical conditions in which the incident occurred, as the spiritual significance of what Sir Peter discovered.

Sir Peter Horsley was, at the time, equerry to His Royal Highness the Duke of Edinburgh. One of his tasks was quietly to investigate credible UFO reports and keep Prince Philip informed of his findings. In fulfilling this duty, he spoke with high-ranking officials, including the Commander-in-Chief of Fighter Command at Stanmore, Air Marshal Sir Thomas Pike, who was later to become Chief of the Air Staff. Far from debunking the matter, which would have been in keeping with the public position of the government, Sir Thomas admitted to Sir Peter that he was concerned about UFO reports. He confirmed that reports were being examined in both Fighter Command and the Ministry of Defence, and that the United States defense authorities were also concerned. One of the many sightings Sir Peter investigated was an object said by Air Force personnel to be traveling at a thousand miles per hour. It is easy to see why, privately, they were taking UFOs very seriously indeed, despite the official stance.

Sir Peter's fascinating encounter with what he took to be an alien visitor occurred in 1954, after he was introduced to a General Martin by the quaintly titled Gentleman Usher to the Sword of State, who was himself a retired Air Chief Marshal, Sir Arthur Barratt. General Martin arranged for Sir Peter to meet a lady, a Mrs Markham, at her apartment in Smith Street in Chelsea, a fashionable part of London. There, in a poorly lit room, he was introduced to Mr Janus, who sat in a deep chair by a not very warm fire, and who claimed to be from another world. Mr Janus asked Sir Peter about his UFO research, informing him with an unusual directness that he would like to meet Prince Philip. Before Sir Peter could respond fully with his concerns about security and so on in arranging such a meeting, Mr Janus responded to these thoughts in what could best be described as a telepathic manner. He demonstrated throughout the encounter what Sir Peter felt was an extraordinary ability to read his thoughts before Sir Peter could express them verbally.

Mr Janus proceeded to provide further background to his request. He spoke of a time when humanity would be able to explore the solar system and beyond; of traveling at the speed of light and even faster than this; of the possibility of gaining mastery over death; of robot and computer-controlled spaceships; and of discovering fields of gravity and antigravity where objects could travel across space and even other universes with different space and time formulae. These concepts are not unfamiliar to us now—they are the stuff of modern science as well as science fiction—but they were far removed from the science of 1954.

Mr Janus went on to discuss what he considered to be more important than the science of space travel—namely, the spirit of man and the universal designer. He spoke of belief in God as being age-old and inherent in even the most primitive people from opposite ends of the Earth. He made the key point that if space travel was conducted for the motive of material gain, it would achieve nothing, but if it was conducted for spiritual reasons, it would lead to a deeper understanding of God. He spoke of a golden age in the future when, providing humanity survives, the greatest advances would be in the development of the mind.

He talked of life throughout the universe, much of it more advanced than our own, and asserted that the humanoid form was not peculiar to the human race. He spoke of races who had overcome the urge to kill and fight wars, and had instead come to love all life, especially humanoid life. They had developed the power of will, and advanced sufficiently to be able to dispense with their physical bodies altogether. They were capable of integrating into the one great universal intelligence, which seems to be akin to the Buddhist concept of nirvana. He spoke of the creator, and the importance of prayer and collective willpower as the essential links to this source. Significantly, he said that these views do not contradict any of the great religious books and that there are many different paths to the same destination. This spiritual approach, he said, is the valid motivating principle behind space travel.

He claimed that the number of visitors who come to Earth from space is a tiny fraction of those who exist. They come to learn about a primitive and hostile race. Most of the vehicles, he said, are robot-controlled space probes, but some of them are manned. He answered the question of why they don't land openly by pointing to the damage done by some of our explorers visiting more primitive cultures. He basically said, though not in these words, that the world was not ready for such a landing. He went on to describe how specific contacts have been made, with great care, through history, and said that this would continue. Finally, he spoke of the visitors' mental abilities, extrasensory powers, and ability to operate in different dimensions.

Sir Peter wrote down his recollections of this meeting immediately after it happened, so we can take it as being an accurate account of what he experienced that day. He reported it to his superiors, but was in two minds about informing the security authorities, whose reaction to such a claim was unpredictable. He wondered whether these security concerns had been "picked up" by Mr Janus, who became mysteriously uncontactable. General Martin became distant and Mrs Markham went away in a hurry, leaving no sign of life in her apartment. Sir Peter never saw any of them again. However, he was, he says, changed by the experience at a profound spiritual level. He saw God in a new light as being a universal and not just a biblical figure, as he had before. He described how he had discovered a much greater intellectual peace as a result of this encounter with the powerful and hypnotic Mr Janus. It is strange to think that while Sir Peter's memoirs containing his account of this extraordinary encounter are, to the best of my knowledge, now out of print, books that focus on the personal and romantic lives of historical figures are readily available, with new ones being commissioned all the time. In a way, that says it all about priorities in our world—and some people wonder why UFOs don't land openly on Earth for all to see!

In the article in the *Sun* on this encounter, I was quoted as saying, "It must have taken courage finally to admit to this contact." Yes it must, but it would have taken far greater courage to admit it openly forty-three years earlier, when it happened. In England the same year, 1954, another man was bold enough to weather the storm of ridicule from public and press alike— George King. He too had a close encounter with an alien being. It happened in his apartment in Maida Vale, London, five miles from Chelsea, as he described in his book, *You Are Responsible!*:

"Prepare yourself! You are to become the voice of Interplanetary Parliament."

That was the simple and precise Command I received one sunny Saturday morning in May 1954. The crisp tones of the voice which uttered the words, coming as it did from apparently empty space in my little flat in London, brought me to a state of shocked immobility. There was no mistaking the meaning of the message or its importance. Nor was there anything eerie about it, for Sunshine and eeriness do not seem to go together.

I had been a student of Yoga for too long to consider that I was a victim of my own imagination. Yoga teaches the pupil that imagination is an energy which, when controlled, becomes transmuted into a great creative force. Having diligently practised this great science for many years, the reader can be assured that I could not easily fall prey to any flight of uncontrolled imaginative fancy.

How many of us can perform good sailing tactics within a sheltered estuary, yet shiver when the captain says: "Now you are ready to take her out to sea, my lad."

That night, the wonderful opaque curtain which is sleep, could not be drawn across the window of my turbulent thoughts. However, by Sunday morning, the somewhat threadbare carpet seemed little the worse for the extra traffic which frequently passed over it during my nocturnal wanderings.

With dawn came the realisation that, that which cannot be rejected must be accepted. Although I had considered the Command from all possible angles, the one thing I could not do was to reject it. The sages from the East have a profound philosophy which governs the student's acceptance of all their teachings. It is: first, read the theory; second, apply this to the mind; and third, act upon that which is acceptable to the consciousness.

I would like to emphasise that it was not the method by which the Command had been given which disturbed me—the Bible records many such happenings—but the fact that, in order to obey it, I should have to give up another line of metaphysical study just when the answer to an important problem seemed imminent. Moreover, a few valiant helpers who possessed humanitarianism as a common factor, all believed that this answer would be of priceless value to suffering mankind. Indeed, we believed that we were on the verge of discovering a new method of cancer treatment which could cure certain forms of this malignant scourge. Nevertheless, this Command came out of the blue in such a way that no receiver could do anything else but listen and obey.

What use is the most carefully predetermined route on a chart in the face of a violent whirlwind? In this case, a whirlwind produced by the cold, unfeeling march of mathematics into unknown skies—skies from which oft-times rained a killer dust to blot out the benign face of the life-giving Sun. It was soon made clear that a drastic measure was necessary in order to meet a grave emergency. For, after spending many hours discussing an enforced change of direction with my immediate associates without obtaining the type of confirmation required, I retreated into contemplation and meditation.

On the following Sunday evening I was somewhat startled by the entrance of another man into my rooms. As is the general practice before attempting meditation, I always carefully lock the door. This had not deterred my visitor who, I discovered later from his method of exit, had obviously walked straight through the door. I recognised him immediately as an Indian Swami of world renown. I am not permitted to divulge his name nor much of what passed, but any lingering doubts I harboured, as to whether the intended healing investigation should take second-place to the previous Saturday's happening, were soon dispelled.

My visitor was a great Yogi Adept, who had projected himself in a more subtle state than what is generally known as the physical body; though he looked real enough; even the boards beneath his feet creaked as he crossed the room. To be in His presence was an experience too wonderful to describe, and until now this has been a precious secret locked up with my most cherished memories.

"It is not for you to judge whether you are worthy to be chosen, my son," said this great Swami. He could obviously read my thoughts, and apparently knew that a feeling of personal unworthiness, for what was obviously a large undertaking, had troubled me for days. He had taken a seat facing me and every line of his face and every inch of his spotlessly white robe was perfectly distinct to me. Even the chair had creaked slightly as he sat down. I had often read about feats performed by the Masters of the East, who could project themselves for thousands of miles in a flash, and appear as life-like as if they had just alighted from an aeroplane. But this was the first time I had ever witnessed such a feat performed by someone whom I knew to be very much alive.

His voice was gentle but had a peculiar penetrating property. "The real necessities of the present age," he declared, "brought about by the unfeeling march of science into the realms of the atom on the one hand, and the wrong thought and action of the masses on the other hand, can only be met by those few who are ready to tune into the emanations now being sent on to this Earth and become the servants of the Cosmic Masters. You are only one of many called upon to prepare yourself for the coming conflict between the materialistic scientist, who has arrived at his conclusions by the cold application of mathematics and the occult scientist who has arrived at his conclusions through the recognition that God is all. Pray, be still, meditate and open the doors of your heart and mind to the precious waters of Truth."

After saying these things, my instructor gave me further Initiation into a certain Yogi exercise, the careful practice of which brings about an ability to travel from the physical body in such a way that full memory of all the experiences gained are retained by the traveller. He also stated that those people best fitted to form a group of willing helpers would be brought into my orbit. I was informed that I should receive a letter from a school of Yoga in London, which I should attend for some months and that I should diligently practise the exercises taught there.

The Swami, having imparted this information, bowed with the politeness of a race which enjoyed an advanced culture when ancient Britons still painted themselves with woad. Then he made his exit by walking straight through my locked door. I dashed to open it immediately, but the long corridor outside was deserted. My friend from the East had disappeared.

This was the spur to action. As it was necessary to set up a group to help in the coming campaign, I gave this formation all my spare time attention. This was to be a specialised group of workers who would be willing to devote hours of their valuable leisure time to help one person to produce the goods. They had to have full belief in the somewhat mysterious project and at the same time be knowledgeable in the basic aspects of occult and contemplative practice. On the face of it, even as few as half a dozen such people would be difficult to meet, but the task seemed to work itself out. In fact, I was able to describe these people a full week before I met them for the first time.

Meanwhile I was invited to a school of Yoga in London by a letter which came out of the blue. The hours spent in the exercises and prana-yama (a system whereby the universal life force is controlled through deep breathing and breath control) yielded good results. Quite soon after the deliverance of the Command, I was able to tune in and receive telepathically, information which was relayed over millions of miles of etheric space.

What a contrast between the experiences of Dr King and Sir Peter Horsley, which occurred within months—possibly even days—of each other. It seems that the beings from other worlds had a variable strategy, depending on whom they were contacting. Approaches to one source would be made in one way, and to another in a different way. Dr King, an exceptionally advanced individual from a spiritual point of view, chose to work as a taxi driver so that he could devote himself to yoga and metaphysical studies. Sir Peter Horsley, who would not claim to have reached a high level of spiritual attainment, held an extremely prominent position within the British establishment. The former bravely set out to fulfill his mission for the Cosmic Masters; the latter admitted to being in two minds about how he should respond to this contact at the time, never passed the information on to Prince Philip, but finally revealed what had happened in the final years of his life.

Dr King faced the ridicule and mockery engendered by the conservative climate of the mid 1950s and pronounced his claim of a contact with an interplanetary being openly and without fear. As an advanced practitioner of yoga and mediumship, he was able to receive communications telepathically, which he did, often in front of large audiences, at Caxton Hall, just down the road from the Houses of Parliament. There he would be given, among other things, forecasts of upcoming flying saucer activity on specific dates and in specific places, and many of these visitations were later verified by independent witnesses. His many contacts and the evidence for them will be described more fully in Chapters 8 and 9, but I should give at least one example of why I am so sure that Dr King received telepathic communications from alien beings. That is surely a claim that demands some further justification. So, here is a case with which I was personally involved while I worked, in a voluntary capacity, as The Aetherius Society's press officer in 1976.

The Society's journal, *Cosmic Voice*, Issue No. 16 June–July 1958, had reported in some detail a nuclear accident that had taken place in the Soviet Union. This information was given to Dr King telepathically on April 18 1958 by interplanetary beings who described the event as occurring recently. The incident was referred to in *Cosmic Voice* as a very serious one in which hundreds of workers at a Russian atomic establishment had been killed. Eighteen years later, in 1976, the highly respected international scientific journal *New Scientist* published an exclusive article by the exiled Soviet scientist, historian, and dissident Dr Zhores Medvedev. In it, he disclosed the hitherto generally unknown fact that there had been a disaster at a nuclear fuel reprocessing plant at Mayak in the province of Chelyabinsk in the Urals. This had occurred sometime in late

1957, with its effects becoming increasingly apparent in early 1958, and hundreds of deaths and thousands of injuries were estimated to have been caused. It had been covered up successfully for eighteen years, and even when the story broke, the British atomic authority denied that any such event had been detected by them.

In the beautiful Devon countryside, Dr King had been informed of this event by an alien communicator and was confident enough of his facts, based only on this communication, to publish it in a journal that was sent all over the world. Although this issue of *Cosmic Voice* is now out of print, several original copies remain extant. I must admit that I was much more naive in 1976 than I am today. I honestly believed that this would be regarded as sufficient evidence to at least warrant a serious investigation of The Aetherius Society's claims by an open-minded media. I realize now that there are two kinds of truth—that which is compatible with the prejudices of the day, and that which is not.

My first port of call was the BBC. I contacted a reporter on the main lunchtime national radio news program, who seemed genuinely interested and wanted to see a copy of *Cosmic Voice* No. 16. I rushed over to Broadcasting House where he duly checked the journal, comparing it with the *New Scientist* revelation. He told me that if I could get Dr Medvedev to confirm specific key facts in his story that directly supported the interplanetary communication delivered eighteen years earlier, I had proved the basis of The Aetherius Society's claims. He recorded an interview with me, which he said he would keep until I had seen Dr Medvedev to verify these facts.

Sure enough, I managed to track down Dr Medvedev later that day at a college in London, and he agreed to be interviewed by me on a portable tape recorder. I did not inform him of the cosmic connection with the nuclear disaster he had just revealed because I did not want to prejudice the interview in any way. I simply asked him the key questions the BBC reporter had wanted me to verify, and recorded his answers, which confirmed the information received by Dr King. I immediately phoned the BBC—by now it was late afternoon—to speak to the reporter, and that's when it all started to unravel. Some readers may find the following facts hard to believe, and I can sympathize with them. All I can say is that they are true.

At first, I was informed that no one had heard of the reporter in question. Later I was told that there may have been someone of that name, but if so, he was only a temporary employee and had now left. Bear in mind that I had been in the building just hours earlier and recorded an interview in a studio for the BBC. Nobody had any idea where the tape of this interview might be, and they certainly were not interested in covering this story. I was starting to discover the machinations of the cover-up, which stretched its tentacles into the media as well as government. Some years later it was finally admitted that there had been a "D" notice on UFOs at that time, i.e. an official government order that prevented certain parts of the media from releasing UFO information. Revealing the truth to the public about the cosmic communication Dr King received concerning the Russian atomic accident seemed dead in the water, but I continued to pester the *New Scientist*'s London office for a couple of years. Finally, on April 27 1978, tucked away in a small corner of the magazine, they admitted that they had been "scooped by a UFO."

The story of the nuclear accident has been extensively covered in the media, especially on the radio, in recent years, reaching millions of listeners all over the world, but at the time, when it was front-page news, nobody would touch the provable story that Dr King had published the story almost twenty years before any of them. I remember one of the more candid journalists from a national, daily newspaper trying to educate me out of my naivety a few years later. "We're not here to publish the truth," he said. "We're here to publish the truth our readers want to read about." Their first priority is, after all, to sell papers. Much of the time, truthful revelations and public interest coincide in the media, and then they can do their job brilliantly. At other times—such as this one—that just isn't the case.

Dr King spoke openly of government cover-ups of UFO information, including in Britain. This does not seem like a brave thing to do nowadays when audiences laugh out loud at cabinet ministers on TV who claim to be honest. But in the 1950s, politicians carried enormous respect, and to say they were lying or withholding information was still a radical thing to do. He spoke in public of a silence group, as did the interplanetary beings who communicated through him. This mysterious organization was said to operate throughout the world for the purpose of preventing the public from hearing the truth about UFOs and their controllers. It went further than denial, and pursued a policy of fabrication as well, building on the fear of horrific aliens as they were so often depicted in science-fiction films of the time. According to Dr King's interplanetary communicators, the silence group would go to any lengths to give the impression that aliens were belligerent, even using actors to impersonate them.

Dr King's cosmic communicators also made it very clear that the plan to prevent the release of UFO data would fail, and so it has, thanks to all those who have campaigned long and hard for it, a campaign that still continues. Dr King organized a public rally in Trafalgar Square in London as long ago as 1958, calling for the truth about UFOs to be revealed, and a few others around the world were also brave enough to speak out. For a government to look honest while admitting that the public have been lied to for decades about UFOs is hardly a spin doctor's dream scenario. Trying to look competent and in charge while revealing details of advanced spacecraft, the origins and technology of which you don't understand, is a veritable PR nightmare. We know far more than we did, but have we really been told the whole truth even now?

CHAPTER 3

X-files, cover-ups, and downright lies

All truth passes through three stages.
First, it is ridiculed. Second, it is
violently opposed. Third, it is accepted
as being self-evident.

Arthur Schopenhauer

A view long-held by conspiracy theorists is that those who talk don't know, and those who know don't talk. There is another theory, of course, that many of those who have talked have lied, but for all the widespread criticism and confusion surrounding UFOs, some facts have emerged about the sophisticated program of disinformation in which governments have engaged.

In case this sounds far-fetched, you only have to think back five hundred years to the revolutionary work of Copernicus, who pioneered the idea that the Earth revolved around the Sun and not the other way around. Today this sounds obvious, but then it was groundbreaking to the point of being heretical. It has to be remembered that the establishment of those days was based as much around the church as it was around the state. Copernicus was himself ordained into the church, taking up the post of canon at Frauenburg Cathedral. The idea of the Sun and planets revolving around the Earth was sacrosanct, in both ecclesiastical and scientific terms. First formulated by Aristotle, and later defined in more detail by Ptolemy, the idea had prevailed for some 1,800 years, almost without challenge. The church had accepted it wholesale and incorporated it into its dogmas, so vigorously enforced by the all too unholy Inquisition. When Copernicus began to realize that the Sun was at the center of planetary motion and the Earth rotated around it once a year, he was up against the full force of the framework of conditioning that prevailed at that time. His revolutionary *Commentariolus*, outlining his views, was too dangerous to publish and was circulated among his friends only. His main work, *De Revolutionibus Orbium Coelestium* (*On the Revolutions of the Heavenly Spheres*) was finally published in 1543, just before his death, and was immediately banned by the Catholic church.

Galileo later took up the ideas, and in 1632 published *Dialogue* concerning the two chief world systems—Ptolemaic and Copernican. In this, he ridiculed the Ptolemaic view of an Earth-centric universe, and supported the Copernican idea. The Catholic Inquisition was so affronted by this work that Galileo was threatened with torture, and forced to renounce the Copernican system. It is extraordinary to think that Galileo's book remained on the Catholic church's banned list until as late as 1835, and for the great crime of publishing the truth about the cosmos, Galileo remained under house arrest for the rest of his life. This is just an illustration of how concepts that fly in the face of the dogma of the day will be rejected and opposed vigorously by the establishment.

Today, it is not the iniquities of the Inquisition that we are up against, but rather the sinister machinery of lying government institutions. These institutions would be perfectly capable of deceiving the world about UFOs if they considered it in their interests to do so. If they cannot convince us that UFOs are figments of our imagination, they could well decide to try to contaminate the truth with fearful stories of hostile interference in the lives of ordinary people by alien visitors. There has been a culture of cover-up, if only to protect the government in power from exposing their ignorance and inability to answer fundamental questions, such as "Who are they?," "Are they friendly?," and "When will they land?" Sooner or later the truth will out. As Abraham Lincoln reputedly said: "You can fool some of the people all of the time, and all of the people some of the time, but you cannot fool all of the people all of the time."

Information has trickled out from government departments under sustained pressure from activists. Much of the material released has been incidental and inconclusive but just occasionally researchers have stumbled across something of real consequence and significance. Among the most fascinating examples of a genuine X-file is a document that was released under the US Freedom of Information Act on December 14 1978. To the best of my knowledge, I was among the first to bring this document to the UK after it was sent to me by a journalist at the *Washington Post* shortly after its release. The result of a lawsuit brought by the Arizona-based UFO organization Ground Saucer Watch against the CIA, the document can easily be found now on the internet and elsewhere. I regard it as particularly significant, not so much because it proves that so-called X-files really exist, but more for the light it throws upon the spiritual nature of UFOs. It indicates beyond doubt that the controllers of UFOs have a mastery over mind and matter that is foreign to Earth technology. It reads as follows:

A At about 12.30 a.m. on September 19 1976 the [deleted] received four telephone calls from citizens living in the Shemiran area of Tehran, saying that they had seen strange objects in the sky. Some reported a kind of bird-like object while others reported a helicopter with a light on. There were no helicopters airborne at that time. After he told the citizens it was only stars and had talked to Mehrabad Tower, he decided to look for himself. He noticed an object in the sky similar to a star [but] bigger and brighter. He decided to scramble an F-4 from Shahrokhi AFB to investigate.

B At 0130 hrs on the 19th the F-4 took off and proceeded to a point about 40nm (nautical miles) north of Tehran. Due to its brilliance, the object was easily visible from 70 miles away. As the F-4 approached a range of 25nm, he lost all instrumentation and communications (UHF and intercom). He broke off the intercept and headed back to Shahrokhi. When the F-4 turned away from the object and apparently was no longer a threat to it, the aircraft regained all instrumentation and communications. At 0140 hrs a second F-4 was launched. The backseater acquired a radar lock-on at 27nm. 12 o'clock high position with the VC (rate of closure) at 150 nmph. As the range decreased to 25nm, the object moved away at a speed that was visible on the radar score and stayed at 25nm.

c The size of the radar return was comparable to that of a 707 tanker. The visual size of the object was difficult to discern because of its intense brilliance. The light that it gave off was that of flashing strobe lights arranged in a rectangular pattern and alternating blue, green, red, and orange in color. The sequence of the lights was so fast that all the colors could be seen at once. The object and the pursuing F-4 continued on a course to the south of Tehran when another brightly lighted object, estimated to be one half to one third the apparent size of the moon, came out of the original object. This second object headed straight toward the F-4 at a very fast rate of speed. The pilot attempted to fire an AIM-9 missile at the object but at that instant his weapons control panel went off and he lost all communications (UHF and interphone). At this point the pilot initiated a turn and negative G dive to get away. As he turned, the object fell in trail at what appeared to be about 3-4nm. As he continued in his turn away from the primary object, the second object went to the inside of his turn, then returned to the primary object for a perfect rejoin.

D Shortly after the second object joined up with the primary object, another object appeared to come out of the other side of the primary object going straight down, at a great rate of speed. The F-4 crew had regained communications and the weapons control panel, and watched the object approach the ground, anticipating a large explosion. This object appeared to come to rest gently on the earth and cast a very bright light over an area of about 2-3 kilometers.

The crew descended from their altitude of 26m to 15m and continued to observe and mark the object's position. They had some difficulty in adjusting their night visibility for landing so after orbiting Mehrabad a few times they went out for a straight in landing. There was a lot of interference on the UHF and each time they passed through a mag. bearing of 150 degrees from Mehrabad they lost their communications (UHF and interphone) and the INS fluctuated from 30 degrees to 50 degrees. The one civil airliner that was approaching Mehrabad during this same time experienced communications failure in the same vicinity (Kilo Zulu) but did not report seeing anything. While the F-4 was on a long final approach the crew noticed another cylinder-shaped object (about the size of a T-bird at 10m) with bright steady lights on each end and a flasher in the middle. When queried, the tower stated there was no other known traffic in the area. During the time that the object passed over the F-4 the tower did not have a visual on it but picked it up after the pilot told them to look between the mountains and the refinery.

E During daylight the F-4 crew was taken out to the area in a helicopter where the object apparently had landed. Nothing was noticed at the spot where they thought the object landed (a dry lake bed) but as they circled off to the west of the area, they picked up a very noticeable beeper signal. At the point where the return was the loudest was a small house with a garden. They landed and asked the people within if they had noticed anything strange last night. The people talked about a loud noise and a very bright light like lightning. The aircraft and area where the object is believed to have landed are being checked for possible radiation. More information will be forwarded when it becomes available.

This document concerns the activities of the then Imperial Iranian Air Force, which at that time worked in close conjunction with the USA. When it was released, the media focused very much on the cover-up that was being perpetrated by world governments about UFOs, which became known as "the Cosmic Watergate"—a reference to the exposure of President Nixon's systematic lies. What is more interesting about this document is what it tells us about the psychology behind the UFOs and those who control them. Clearly, there was an attempt to fire a missile at the UFO. At that exact instant the weapons control panel on the jet was demobilized and it was prevented from doing so. Later, when the UFO had performed further maneuvers, it was observed that the control panel was activated again—possibly when the jet was out of range of the UFO. The implications of this are vast. How could the controllers of the UFO have known the intentions of the pilot at that exact moment, and how could they have remotely demobilized the weapons control panel, seemingly activating it again when it was in no position to do harm?

However, the CIA document reveals something of far greater importance than just the fact that a major superpower attempted to chase a UFO and fire missiles at it. Even though the pilot had hostile intent toward the UFO, according to this report, and was willing to fire at it, the controllers of what must have been a spacecraft were benign. Based on the description of its capabilities in this document, they could easily have retaliated, damaging the jet if they had wanted to do so. The fact that they did not was surely a demonstration of forgiveness—not returning like for like. Instead, they gently took control of the situation so that no harm was inflicted upon any party. Can you imagine the same kind of spirituality being demonstrated by the armed forces of different governments on this planet toward each other?

This incident is unusual but not unique in its disclosure of a UFO being pursued by a military jet. In 1991, for example, the Belgian Ministry of Defence released radar tapes from two Belgian Air Force F-16s, which had been scrambled to follow a UFO in March 1990. This object had been detected by four ground-based radar stations, and had been seen by police officers and many citizens. The tapes were sensational, showing digital readouts of exceptionally high altitude and extraordinary speed changes made by the UFO. Even more extraordinary was the lack of media coverage given to this highly credible government release. It subsequently emerged in a letter from Malcolm Rifkind, while he was the UK Secretary of State for Defence, to Lord Hill-Norton, former Admiral of the Fleet and Chief of Defence Staff, that the ministry was not informed of this incident by Belgium at the time it occurred. If true, this shows the total inadequacy of world governments to grapple with the most important phenomenon of our times.

Another very revealing government document describes the landing of a UFO and the alien being who emerged from it during an event that was witnessed by a large number of people. This is not a story someone has just come up with, or an account that has been passed down through various people in verbal and written form. It is a government record released just twenty years ago.

The former Soviet press agency TASS (Telegraph Agency of the Soviet Union) reported it in 1989 and released it along with other UFO papers in the spirit of President Gorbachev's "glasnost"—his new policy of openness and transparency regarding the activities of government institutions, and a desire to provide some freedom of information. What TASS didn't reckon on was the inbuilt skepticism and prejudice of the western media who, for the most part, either ignored or ridiculed it.

I was personally involved in bringing these papers to the attention of the media in Britain at the time, and was in touch with a journalist in Moscow who told me of the TASS representative's surprise and dismay at the way this material was treated, especially in the USA and Britain. The same journalists who were hanging on every word released by TASS about the disarmament negotiations between the USA and USSR at the time, faithfully reproducing statements that were released about this, would not consider reproducing statements from the same source about a UFO landing in full view of a crowd of people, and an alien being demonstrating what can only be described as paranormal powers. Having said that, there were those who did report this highly significant incident as described in the TASS documents, and all credit to them. One was Gloria Hunniford's show on ITV in the UK on which I was invited to appear as a guest. The first time I was edged out at the last minute by an interview with the infamous Robert Maxwell about the launch of his new newspaper, but I was invited back and the facts went out fairly and accurately. However, the full implications of this outstanding event could not be fully explored in the short time allocated on any television chat show. The TASS report is reproduced here in full:

10 Oct 89 Soviet Newspaper Confirms UFO Report (478) MOSCOW

Recent reports about the landing of aliens in the Russian city of Voronezh were confirmed in today's issue of *Sovetskaya Kultura*.

The aliens landed on a warm autumn evening on September 27, the paper said. Two boys and a girl from a local school, Vasya Surin, Zhenya Blinov and Yulya Sholokhova, were in the city park. The place was crowded, with several dozen people waiting at a nearby bus stop. The boys were playing football.

At half past six, they saw a pink light shining in the sky and then spotted a ball of a deep-red colour about 10 meters in diameter. The ball circled the park for some time above the earth and disappeared. It reappeared a few moments later and hovered above the park.

A crowd of onlookers rushed to the site, the paper said. They could clearly see a hatch opening in the lower part of the ball and a humanoid in the opening. The alien was about three meters high, had three eyes, was clad in silvery overalls and "boots" the colour of bronze and had a disk on its chest. The humanoid looked the place over. The hatch closed and the ball began to descend. "The object" then landed, according to the paper. The hatch opened again and two creatures came out, one apparently a robot.

The first one said something and a shining triangle, 30 by 50 centimeters in size, appeared on the ground and soon disappeared. The alien touched the robot's body, and it started moving in a mechanical way.

One of the boys started screaming with fear. The alien looked at him and the boy fell silent, unable to move. The alien's eyes were shining. The onlookers screamed. After a little while the ball and the creatures disappeared.

In about five minutes, the ball and the three-eyed humanoid could be seen again. The alien had what looked like a gun by his side—a tube about 50 centimeters long. He directed the thing at the 16-year-old boy and the latter disappeared. The alien went inside the ball, which immediately took off. At the same time the boy reappeared.

"It is hard to believe what happened," the paper's Voronezh correspondent, E. Yefremov, writes. "It is harder yet to explain, but there is no doubt that something really happened."

The UFO landing was witnessed by several people. Residents of Putilin Street in Voronezh said they repeatedly saw a UFO from September 23 to 29.

Militia officers and reporters interviewed the children and those who saw the anomaly. There are no contradictions in the descriptions of the ball or of the aliens' actions. All the children who saw the alien craft are still afraid. The local section that studies anomalies is investigating the incident, the paper said. The section includes scientists, physicists and biologists.

TASS—Telegraph Agency of the Soviet Union

As with the document released by the CIA, it is not so much the sensationalist aspect of this report that interests me as the underlying spiritual message. There is technology at work here, which demonstrates yet again that UFOs and their occupants have a control over matter that is literally light years ahead of our science. The crowd was shown, through an indisputable demonstration of power, that these beings could easily do damage if they wished to. They could control a boy with a glance, they could even make him disappear and reappear, and yet nobody was harmed, and they left peacefully without forcing anyone to do or believe anything they did not wish to.

You may be wondering why none of these very revealing documents led the news bulletins on radio and television or dominated the front pages of the press, or perhaps, by now, you are not surprised. One story that did hit the headlines was an incident that, for me, took place much closer to home, in Suffolk. I remember well the autumn morning in 1983 when I received a phone call from Dr King. I was staying at a hotel in Carlisle on the way back from Scotland. Dr King was calling from London to alert me to a story he had just seen in one of the Sunday papers. Apparently, a Member of Parliament had raised the matter of a UFO landing near a US Air Force base in Woodbridge, Suffolk, in 1980. I rushed back to London to investigate the matter further. I remember speaking to a female officer at the Bentwaters Royal Air Force base near Woodbridge, who started to admit that something had happened, until she was instructed, during the call, to say nothing more to me. The whole incident was later described in a book by Georgina Bruni, *You Can't Tell the People*. This title was based on a statement about UFOs that the author claimed was made to her by the ex-Prime Minister Margaret Thatcher on May 21 1997—you must get your facts right, and you can't tell the people.

The incident occurred in Christmas week of 1980 at the Bentwaters and Woodbridge bases, where approximately 12,000 US Air Force personnel were located. It was one of the largest NATO complexes in Europe. Bentwaters is bordered by Rendlesham Forest and some say a nuclear arsenal was located at this base. Certainly, the personnel there were highly trained. It is difficult to ascertain the true facts about what exactly happened because a cover-up kicked in, and because not all reports of the incident concur with each other on every detail. What follows is a summary of some of the salient points as they have been reported, although there are some inconsistencies for the above reasons. What is not in doubt is that this was an outstanding UFO experience.

At 3 a.m. on December 26 1980, Airman John Burroughs was the duty officer patrolling the air base. It was a cold night with a little bit of fog. Sergeant Bud Steffens arrived in a truck, collected Burroughs, and they drove around the edge of Rendlesham Forest. Steffens noticed a strange light with a weird glow. Burroughs saw it too and described it as different colored lights blinking on and off. The two men called the Flight Desk from a secure line, which meant that it was routed to Central Security Control (CSC). The shift commander despatched Staff Sergeant Jim Penniston, who arrived within minutes at East Gate. Penniston saw, in the woods, a multicolored object, which looked to him as though it was an aircraft that had crashed. He called CSC for permission to investigate what he took to be a crash.

Burroughs and Penniston drove toward the light, and when the vehicle could be taken no farther, they continued on foot. As they came closer to the mysterious object, the interference on their radios increased. Penniston described feeling what seemed to be an electric charge through his clothes, face, and hair. There was no smell of smoke as they came into a clearing, but just a blinding white light. As they came closer still, the light dimmed. The craft was described as being triangular in shape and estimated at nine feet wide by eight feet high. The surface of the craft was smooth with no visible cockpit, engines, or any other discernible features, such as landing gear. Although visible, it was soundless. In what was claimed to be an original statement, Penniston was quoted as saying that the object was mechanical and was producing red and blue light. The blue light was projecting under the object, lighting up the area directly underneath and extending for a meter or two. He and Burroughs proceeded after the object as it zigzagged through the woods, and eventually they lost sight of it.

In later interviews, Penniston described how he touched the object, which he said was warm but not hot. Lights seemed to be emitted from the fabric of the craft in a way he could not explain, and he also noticed strange symbols on it. Suddenly, a blinding flash of light came from the object, and it moved up over the trees and away at a phenomenal speed. According to Penniston, it happened in the blink of an eye. He also noticed another, very different flash of light through the trees from a nearby lighthouse. As soon as the craft had left, their radios, which had ceased to function, worked perfectly again. Penniston also said that indentations were left by the craft in the form of three round impressions in symmetrical patterns in the ground, roughly ten feet apart and each one about two to three inches thick.

Following this incident, the men were debriefed. Penniston says he was told that it would not be a good career move to report everything as it happened, so he was reluctant to do so, and gave a sanitized version. He says that he received a thinly veiled warning that sometimes things are best left alone. This explains some of the contradictions that have emerged in some of the accounts. But that was not the end of the story.

On the night of either December 28 or 29 (it was reported as both) more UFO sightings occurred. Deputy Base Commander Lt Col Charles Halt made a record of these encounters two weeks later in a memo to the UK Ministry of Defence. The memo was released to Citizens Against UFO Secrecy (CAUS) in the United States in June 1983 under the Freedom of Information Act. Halt was in the Officers' Club when he received a report of a UFO sighting and, collecting a three-man security team, and a small cassette recorder, he went out to Rendlesham Forest to investigate, fully expecting to find a rational explanation. He encountered radio problems, as Penniston and Burroughs had done, and noticed gashes in the bark of trees where the two had been a few nights earlier. Animals in the forest and from a local farm started to become very vocal, making a considerable noise.

Then Halt noticed a bright red, glowing object with a dark center, emitting a yellow color. It moved through the trees horizontally and seemed to drip molten metal, which appeared to form into white pieces. Overhead, an object approached at speed, stopped, and emitted a beam at their feet. The light disappeared and the object sped away. Some believe this beam pinpointed a nuclear storage area at the base. At this point, we are told, Halt's recorder ran out of tape, but he and his team remained in the forest for several hours.

In his memo, Halt describes three star-like objects, two to the north, which were visible for over an hour, and one to the south, which was visible for over two hours and which emitted a beam of light from time to time. Despite the obvious credibility of such witnesses, being trained military personnel, knowledge of receiving any reports about this event was denied by the UK Ministry of Defence, until the memo was released in the USA and the ministry was forced to acknowledge it.

Years later, after retiring from the US Air Force, in a press release dated June 25 2009, Charles Halt went further in his description of the objects he saw in December 1980. He made it clear that the UFOs he saw were, in his view, structured machines moving under intelligent control and operating beyond the realm of anything he had ever seen before or since. He stated that, in his belief, the objects, which he saw at close quarters, were extraterrestrial in origin. He categorically confirmed that the security services of the USA and UK had tried to subvert the significance of what occurred in Rendlesham Forest and had used methods of disinformation to do so.

Other claims have been made in connection with this case. Burroughs is said to have gone to investigate with another airman and seen a blue glow in a field, but as he ran toward it the light disappeared. Former US Air Force security police officer Larry Warren also claims that some form of communication took place with three aliens in humanoid form, a story that is denied by other officers involved. In 2002, declassified files revealed that there had been faulty radar, and date errors and missing information in the files are regarded as highly suspicious by some researchers. Some people, including some of the participants in these incidents, believe that the full truth is still being hidden from the public. A former government official, who at one time worked at the Ministry of Defence in the department that dealt with UFO reports, has been quoted as describing the Rendlesham Forest sightings as the biggest UFO incident of all time. The event has been dubbed the "British Roswell."

There is no denying a cover-up. Witnesses say they were told not to talk about it, and some allege that they were threatened. The photos that were taken were developed in the photo laboratory at the base and apparently came out blank. The public were kept in the dark for almost three years until the story broke in the press, on the day I received the call from Dr King. I remember in some early radio interviews I did with debunkers in the studio, some ludicrous explanations were being given. One astronomer, for example, claimed that the lights, which had been seen by trained experts, were in fact from the nearby lighthouse, the marks in the bark of the trees had been made by a woodcutter, and the indentations in the ground were a result of badgers! It seems absurd now to think that anyone would have the gall to come up with such absurd explanations, but come up with them they did. Not all such people were government stooges, but probably some were.

Classic examples of government stooges are the so-called "Men in Black" (MIB). On occasions, just after convincing UFO sightings or encounters had taken place, witnesses reported being visited by men dressed in dark suits, often with hats and dark glasses. It sounds comical now, and Hollywood has had a ball portraying them, but they were not so amusing at the time to those who said they were visited by them for the purpose of being silenced. I have spoken to credible individuals who claim to have been visited by MIB, in both the UK and New Zealand, who said they felt the intention was to intimidate them. The men generally claimed to come from an unspecified or little-known government department, and would even produce ID to prove it. Sometimes they were said to have threatened the witness with injury to himself or his family if he spoke about his sighting to anybody. It is possible that MIB were indeed government agents, or even actors dressed up by government departments to intimidate witnesses.

However, in probably the best-known MIB case, that of Albert K. Bender, it's likely they were neither of these. The case has become the archetype for experiences of this kind. Bender had founded the International Flying Saucer Bureau, a small organization, in Connecticut, USA, in 1952. Its magazine, *Space Review*, was sent out to just a few hundred subscribers. In October 1953, Bender suspended publication of *Space Review*, having advised his readers to be very cautious about their flying saucer work. He later revealed in a newspaper interview that he had been visited by three men who had frightened him to such an extent that he had closed down his organization and journal. Friends and associates described him as a changed man after this visit. He says that he was lying down in his bedroom when he noticed three figures dressed in black and wearing hats in the room. They informed him that some of his theories about UFOs were correct but that he should cease his work in this field forthwith. Bender attributes certain paranormal qualities to these visitors, including eyes that lit up like lightbulbs and an ability to practice telepathy. Indeed, one possible explanation for MIB is that they personify psychic interference from lower realms of existence. This subject will be explored in more detail in Chapter 7.

Another, more down-to-earth, case is that of Robert Richardson of Toledo, Ohio. In July 1967, he says, he collided with a UFO when driving at night. Unable to halt his car while navigating a bend, he came into contact with the object, which immediately vanished. He says the impact was relatively mild and that he later found a small lump of pewter-colored metal, possibly from the UFO. He reported the incident to the Aerial Phenomena Research Organization. Three days later, two men arrived at his home and started to question him. This was followed a week later by two other men, wearing black suits, who informed him that he had not come into collision with any object and asked him to hand over the metal, threatening him and his wife if he didn't. He was not able to do so because he had already sent the sample to UFO researchers.

One MIB witness I spoke to myself was Jim Templeton of Cumbria, in the North of England. I also interviewed him for LBC radio when I was a guest host for the "Phenomena Files" on that station with Mike Allen. Jim, who worked for the Cumbrian Fire Service in Carlisle, took his wife and daughter for a picnic at a nature resort, Burgh Marsh, on May 24 1964. The occasion was relatively uneventful except for a strange feeling of electricity in the air, rather like that before a thunderstorm. Jim took a photo of his daughter and, when it was developed, found that a tall figure had appeared in the picture, standing a short distance behind the child, wearing what seemed to be a white spacesuit and helmet. The picture was investigated by Kodak and tampering of any kind was ruled out after examination of the negative. This image became known as the Cumbrian, or Cumberland, spaceman. After the photograph was published in a local paper, Jim received a telephone call from someone who said he worked for the government, telling him to drop the matter immediately. Two visitors came to his fire station, wearing the bowler hats that were typical of British civil servants at that time, and claiming to represent Her Majesty's Government. They went with him to the site of the picnic and interrogated Jim about what he had seen there. This story is tame in comparison with some of those that have emerged from the other side of the Atlantic, but nevertheless indicates the alleged attempts by UK government officials at the time to silence witnesses of UFO or alien phenomena.

In February 1967, Colonel George Freeman, Pentagon spokesman for the US Air Force Project Blue Book, was quoted as telling a UFO investigator that strange men dressed in Air Force uniforms and carrying credentials from various government agencies had been silencing UFO witnesses. Colonel Freeman apparently claimed that these men were impostors, who had no connection to the Air Force or the government. It could be, of course, that this was itself a deliberate piece of disinformation, but there is another possibility—namely that they were from a government department so deeply entrenched in secrecy that it was not known or identifiable to an officer such as Colonel Freeman. Whatever the truth of this and reports generally from various parts of the world, MIB were, on occasions, said to be in possession of restricted information, not released to the press and known only to a few investigators and officials.

However, it is not just governments who have tried to suppress or distort the truth. Falsehood can emanate from a very dark place from a spiritual perspective, the work of occult forces from this or a lower realm of existence. In ufology, I believe this is particularly true of the so-called abduction phenomenon, which needs to be treated with great caution. It is not just a matter of whether the claims are true or false, although discrimination is essential, but with abductions it is also a matter of whether, even if they are true experiences, they have anything at all to do with UFOs or extraterrestrial beings.

The investigation of abductions has relied very heavily on the use of hypnosis. Regressive hypnosis has often been regarded as the most efficient method for revealing a forgotten period of time, which could be as short as an hour or two. Psychiatrists and psychologists have often been used to help in this process. The reason for this is that very often those who claim to have experienced abductions do not remember exactly what happened to them. Sometimes they have just discovered that a period of their life is missing, and have no recall of it until memory is triggered in a state of hypnotic trance, which then leads on to extraordinary descriptions of alien abductions.

I must put my cards on the table here and say that, for me, this type of evidence is highly suspect. I am no expert on hypnosis, but I do know that it is open to abuse. Thoughts and ideas may be planted into a subject's mind while in a hypnotic state, and then, when the person is brought out of trance, remain in the consciousness as a supposed memory. Witnesses are not lying but describing what they now believe to have happened. As we all know, in the field of entertainment, this principle is used for the amusement of the audience, when hypnotized subjects genuinely believe they are witnessing something that is not there, or talking to somebody who is in fact somebody else. The practice could be deliberately misused in order to cause confusion within the UFO movement, with the ultimate aim of discrediting it, if any agency wished to do so.

Allegedly, there has even been a case of a fake abductee planted specifically to deceive a professor of psychiatry. The professor proceeded to use hypnosis and was completely taken in, much to his embarrassment. This does not invalidate all claimants, but it certainly raises questions about the authenticity of data gained through hypnotic regression.

I am not suggesting that all those who have claimed abductions are either deliberately or misguidedly deceiving people. There may indeed be genuine cases among the most benign claims but I would refute completely the idea that hostile aliens are abducting individuals who have no memory of these experiences until they are hypnotically regressed. For one thing, hostile aliens would not need to go to these lengths since, if they were able to get that close to our Earth, they could very easily invade it openly. I believe we are protected from hostile alien attacks, and will elaborate on this later in the book. If we were not so protected, we could all have been killed or enslaved quite easily some time ago. However, I also believe that, quite apart from government agencies, there are hostile forces connected with our world who have an interest in suppressing the truth about UFOs.

In a recent lecture that I gave on this subject in the North of England, several well-versed ufologists in the audience were very surprised by the positive tone of my talk. They have become so used to the dark forebodings and pessimistic concepts that have infected the UFO movement over the last couple of decades that they described my more spiritual take on this subject as a virtual ray of light. There could be a very good reason for this negativity among ufologists. Mysticism and the existence of other realms is something I will discuss in depth in Chapter 7, but one cannot do justice to explaining abductions, in my view, without touching on the dark side of psychic phenomena.

Many abduction reports are connected with either the sleep state, lost time, memory blackouts, or trance states of one kind or another. All of these can be conducive elements for paranormal experiences, which have been with us for thousands of years, and are not necessarily connected in any shape or form with alien beings. Whereas the medieval mind might have seen negative entities as hobgoblins, or in a later period as possession cases or poltergeists, perhaps the modern equivalent for some people is alien beings with large skulls and a predilection for sadistic surgical operations. The dark side of occultism, which in my view should be avoided at all costs, all too often uses magic or other methods to gain control over others. Under certain conditions, it would be perfectly possible for a dark force from this or another realm, if they considered it worthwhile, to plant thoughts in people's brains while they slept, or even during a period of limited consciousness while they are awake, which would make them believe quite falsely that they had experienced an alien abduction. It could be a vivid memory for them, or even something that could be extracted through hypnotic regression. I would say that such a force, if powerful enough—and psychic research through the ages does indicate extraordinary events at a physical as well as a mental level—could place a physical implant in a human being, and program them to think that it came from an alien source. Once again, such a happening, backed up by apparent physical evidence, could be corroborated through hypnotic regression.

For those to whom all this sounds very far-fetched, I would strongly recommend in-depth psychic research. Having done numerous radio phone-ins on various stations around the world, I have been surprised by just how many paranormal experiences are taking place in the day-to-day physical lives of ordinary people, who would not describe themselves as being in any way psychic. Many in the UFO movement have gone out of their way to separate their studies from the world of paranormal phenomena, which they regard as questionable. These nuts-and-bolts researchers, as they are sometimes described, have eschewed their more metaphysical counterparts, and in doing so have made, in my opinion, a grave error. Nowhere is this more evident than in the study of abductions, which requires some metaphysical grounding to comprehend the full range of experiences being described.

In addition to a few benign abduction claims that could well be genuine; deliberate hoaxes, perpetrated for either financial gain or the futile quest for "fifteen minutes of fame"; those that are a result of mental health issues; and acts of deliberate deception by governments, or badly motivated individuals, who may be using hypnosis to plant false memories in their subjects—I am suggesting, in a way that has not been explained before in any other book that I know of, that there is another category even more complex than any of these. The people who fall into this category are those who have been programed by dark forces from this, or more likely a lower, realm of existence to believe, and in their minds experience, what they regard as an alien abduction. These experiences are usually of a very harrowing and unpleasant nature, sometimes with long-term consequences. Subjects certainly need therapeutic help, and in some cases psychic and spiritual help as well. Positive steps can be taken to protect yourself from psychic interference. But if there has been a deliberate plan by dark forces to cause confusion and negativity within the UFO movement through abductions, it has, regrettably, been very successful in its implementation.

So what kind of experiences are people claiming to have? Many of the drawings done by so-called abductees are of the typical "grays," an image of an alien that has been widely publicized throughout the world, and taken up by Hollywood and various marketing enterprises. It is, of course, possible that such an entity really does exist on other planets. The type of experience can range from being stopped while driving a vehicle to being transported into an unknown spacecraft and at times allegedly exposed to certain investigatory procedures. Other claimants describe how they have been taken on trips to other worlds in these spacecraft, while yet others say they have had long conversations with the alien beings, who gave them messages to relay to the world, such as appealing to us to stop atomic experimentation and war, and help to bring about peace.

Over the years, many stories have circulated about how or what happens during an abduction. These events have allegedly taken place in the bedroom, with the claimants often seeing "grays" at the end of the bed. In many cases, the claimants have talked about being unable to move or feeling paralyzed, and then finding themselves in a room in what they first may think is a hospital and, when they see the alien entities, realize could be a spacecraft. Many have also reported feeling that they have been either guided or physically made to lie on a table, and subjected to various bodily examinations. In some extreme cases, there have been accounts of implants and samples of fluids being taken from their bodies. Some have reported that, even though the occurrence may have lasted for just a couple of minutes, a longer period of time has elapsed, which cannot be accounted for. This is sometimes referred to as "missing time." Claimed abductions have an average duration of around one to two hours, although in some accounts they last for much longer, even days. These experiences have been reported by people from various walks of life—some who were already believers in UFOs and some who were not.

The first abduction claim of recent times occurred on the night of September 19 1961, when Betty and Barney Hill were returning from a vacation in Canada, traveling to their home to New Hampshire. As they were driving, at around 10.15 p.m., they noticed a light below the moon, and even though they thought it was a satellite or a plane, something about it made them think it worth looking at for longer, and they stopped the car for a while. When they drove on, they continued to watch the object, which seemed to grow in size as well as darting away to the west and then back. They stopped the car again and, through his binoculars, Barney could see lights, which appeared to be just a hundred feet away. Barney decided to try to get closer to the object and claimed he could see figures inside a spacecraft. Becoming frightened, he ran back to Betty in the car and sped off as quickly as he could. Apparently, they heard a beeping noise and when it came a second time, it was followed by a bump, but they carried on driving home. Later, they could not explain various problems they found with the car, or the recurring dreams that Betty started to have ten days after the sighting and which lasted for five days, or the extremely painful back Barney was suffering from. When they were put under hypnotic regression, both Betty and Barney Hill separately talked of being taken into a UFO and undergoing medical examinations before being returned to their car.

Another well-known abduction claim is that of Linda Napolitano (who originally used the name Cortile). She apparently floated out through a closed window of her New York apartment at 3 a.m. on November 30 1989, and was guided into a craft that was hovering over the building. This event was witnessed by two bodyguards who were escorting a high-profile UN statesman through Manhattan. These two bodyguards claimed that they saw a woman, accompanied by what appeared to be alien beings, floating up toward a saucer-shaped object, which they said had lights changing from a bright, reddish orange to whitish blue. Although she seemed to have lost her memory of the actual transportation, when placed under hypnotic regression she recalled being placed on a table inside the craft and being examined, after which she suddenly found herself back in bed at home.

One of the most famous abductions took place in the early evening of November 5 1975. A young woodcutter, Travis Walton, was returning home with his fellow lumberjacks from the Apache-Sitgreaves National Forests in east-central Arizona. One of the men caught sight of a golden glow through the thickets as they drove along the forest trail. On reaching the source of this glow, they found a mysterious craft, and Walton jumped out of the vehicle to take a closer look. The craft appeared to have a metallic hull, and a hum that sounded as though it was made by some sort of machinery came from inside. All of a sudden, an energy beam appeared to shoot out of the spacecraft, lifting Walton up and then forcing him to the ground, at which point his friends, who had remained in the vehicle, drove off in fear for their own safety. According to one report, they waited until they saw a light, which they took to be the object, rising into the sky before returning to the area, but there was no sign of the young woodcutter. Five days later, on November 10, a family member received a phone call from a confused and disorientated Walton. They found him in the phone booth with five days' growth of beard. He could remember only an hour or two of his five-day absence, during which he claimed to have been in a room where he underwent some type of examination.

This hotly disputed case is still mired in controversy, and was the subject of the 1993 movie "Fire in the Sky." A number of polygraph (lie detector) tests were taken by Travis Walton and the lumberjacks who witnessed the incident. Some were passed successfully, although others are contested. Questions have also been raised about Walton's recollection of what happened to him, which was first given in the presence of a hypnotherapist. It is not clear how much of it was real memory, hypnotic regression, or fear-filled imagination after a very traumatic experience. Whatever combination of these elements applies, it is certainly a very significant case and many researchers believe something definitely happened to Travis Walton. Also, the indications are that, if aliens were involved, they were not of hostile intent, since they could easily have seriously damaged or killed Walton if they had wanted to do so. I believe that the vast majority of abduction stories are questionable, to say the very least, and a calculated program of deception by the political and military establishment cannot be discounted.

In a very different context, I had firsthand experience of coming up against the establishment when I was in America in the spring of 1987, working with Dr King. A report came to light that a Japan Airlines (JAL) transportation flight, No. 1628, flying over Alaska on November 17 1986, had been pursued by a UFO. The report was made by the plane's pilot, Captain Kenju-Terauchi.

The Boeing 747 jumbo jet was carrying wine from France to Japan and no passengers were on board, just the pilot and his crew. The pilot described the silhouette of the object, eight miles away, as being like a disk with a ring around it, and estimated it to be huge, dwarfing his airplane. The unknown object had been tracked by radar from the ground and air-traffic control instructed Captain Kenju-Terauchi to try to shake it off, but he was unable to do so. He and his crew observed it for over half an hour, and for hundreds of miles, before it disappeared. They also observed two smaller objects leaving the large one and darting about quickly, occasionally stopping dead still, and noted that the main object performed the well-known feat for an extra-terrestrial spacecraft of "blinking in and out," i.e. disappearing and reappearing. We and others launched a vociferous campaign for the facts to be released to the public, but despite this cast-iron sighting by trained observers, backed up by radar records from air-traffic control, it was like pulling teeth to get the Federal Aviation Administration (FAA) to issue any information about it, and it was followed by the customary attempt to explain it all away.

Years later, on May 9 2001, a public press conference was held at the National Press Club in Washington DC to launch a disclosure project, the idea of which was to discuss restricted information about UFO activity contained in papers that had hitherto been classified by governments around the world. One of the delegates at this conference was John Callahan, who had been FAA Division Chief at the time of the JAL sighting. He revealed that a briefing about this incident had been held at the time by the FAA Administrator, Admiral Engen, which was attended by representatives of the FBI, the CIA, and President Reagan's scientific study team among others. When the meeting concluded, CIA members apparently instructed everyone present that the briefing had never taken place, and the incidents were never recorded. As someone who was at the cutting edge at the time the original report first came to light, I know that all we received from officialdom was a series of denials until they were forced to release some documentation, which was far from the complete story. The pilot himself was forced to take a desk job for a prolonged period and was humiliated for the stance he took in reporting the incident to the press.

Some would say that we are lied to by our political leaders about wars they have embarked upon under our very noses. So any sense of security people may feel from the illusory idea that governments have this matter in hand, and it is not a concern for us, needs to be dispensed with. They do not know the full answers to the great issue of our extraterrestrial visitors, but somewhere in the nooks and crannies of the world's intelligence services they do have far more information than we have been given.

Occasionally, cracks of light have appeared in the wall of denial erected by governments. American astronaut Dr Edgar Mitchell stated openly on *The Oprah Winfrey Show* in 1991 that a lot more is known about extraterrestrials than has been made available to the public. A few years later he went even further than this when he admitted on television that he had met officials from three different countries who had had close encounters with extraterrestrials in the course of their duties. Another American astronaut, Gordon Cooper, put in writing, for a 1978 meeting at the United Nations, that extraterrestrial vehicles and crews are visiting this planet and are more advanced than we are. He later stated that although astronauts are very cautious about revealing their UFO experiences, several of them have had them.

What we have been told is just the tip of a very large iceberg, and it looks as though, in the UK at least, it will stay that way. On December 1 2009, the UK Ministry of Defence (MOD) officially closed its hotline and email address for the public to report UFO sightings. After over fifty years of logging, and occasionally investigating, reported sightings, the ministry has closed its UFO unit on the grounds that it had no "defense value." The BBC announced that £44,000 a year would be saved by moving the officer who had handled these reports to another job. An MOD spokesman added that resources were being focused on the top priority—a front-line war being conducted against the Taliban in Afghanistan. The ministry said that the UFO unit had received thousands of reports, and that none of them had yielded proof of aliens, or any security threat to the UK. Nailing their colors firmly to the fence, the ministry said it had "no opinion on the existence or otherwise of extraterrestrial life." It added that in over fifty years there had not been a single UFO report that gave evidence of a potential threat to the United Kingdom. Therefore there was no defense benefit to be gained from such an investigation and it was inappropriate to use defense resources for this purpose. Any threats to the UK's air space would be spotted by radar checks and dealt with by RAF fighter aircraft.

Perhaps the most revealing admission by the ministry was made in the following statement: "The MOD has no specific capability for identifying the nature of such sightings." There may have been some disingenuousness behind this statement in an attempt, essentially, to pass the buck. Nevertheless, taken at face value it is a candid confession by the defense arm of a leading nation of its total inadequacy to cope with the enormous significance of this phenomenon. Furthermore, the fact that it has not been taken up by any other government department shows a total failure by the political establishment to grapple with UFOs. This is a long way from taking such a vital issue seriously. As Dante put it in his distinctively uncompromising way: "The darkest places in hell are reserved for those who maintain their neutrality in times of moral crisis."

Of course, some people will not believe the MOD's statement for one minute, especially in the year when the number of sightings reported to the ministry more than tripled. On September 20 2009, the editorial of the *Sunday Telegraph*, a very conservative newspaper, stated that at least one Briton every single day has a close encounter. The foremost location for sightings in the UK, and according to some in the world, is the Scottish town of Bonnybridge, just west of Falkirk and not far from Edinburgh—so much so that the surrounding area stretching from Stirling to the outskirts of Scotland's capital city, has been dubbed "the Falkirk Triangle." Hundreds of sightings are reported there every year. One of the local councillors, Billy Buchanan, told me during a radio interview some years ago that there had been many thousands of sightings in this region, and that he himself had taken video footage of UFOs, which had never been disproved. The media have great fun covering this extraordinary confluence of sightings in just one spot, typically including in their headlines the phrase, "Beam me up Scottie!"

Could the number of sightings being witnessed in Bonnybridge and other parts of the UK have set off alarm bells in the corridors of power, causing them to rethink their whole strategy? Was it time to close the book once and for all on any official connection between government departments and the existence of UFOs? Conspiracy theorists believe that since the Freedom of Information Act has forced the UK government to release at least some of its UFO files to the public, this was a way of preventing further releases, should anything come its way. After all, if the official position is that the government does not receive UFO reports, how could anybody apply to have them released?

Whatever the ministry's true intentions—whether it be a sinister plan to continue the cover-up, or whether it be a total failure to recognize the significance of this phenomenon—the UK is left with a government that has totally renounced its responsibility for involvement with UFOs, at least officially. Politicians should not be surprised, after their record, if some people simply don't believe them.

One government that is very open about this issue, according to press reports in 2009, is the government of Bulgaria. Members of the Space Research Institute of the Bulgarian Academy of

Sciences, including the Deputy Director, Lachezar Filipov, said they were engaged in an investigation of contacts with extraterrestrials. They had posed thirty questions and were analyzing crop circles that had appeared around the globe in 2009, where they felt the answers to their questions may lie.

Filipov was quoted as saying that aliens are currently all around us and are watching us all the time. He was adamant that they are not hostile toward us. Rather, they want to help us but we have not advanced enough to establish direct contact with them. He added that such direct contacts would take place in the next ten to fifteen years, but significantly it would happen through telepathy rather than radio waves. There are those, including myself, who would say that this has already happened on our Earth, both in recent times and throughout history.

Filipov went on to make the interesting observation that extraterrestrials are critical of unethical behavior, in reference to human interference in the processes of nature. This chimes with the claims of those contactees who say that extraterrestrials are looking more for a spiritual sign from us than a technological one, and it is this that will trigger closer contact with us. In some ways, it is a shame that the Space Research Institute of the Bulgarian Academy of Sciences is examining crop circles for answers, rather than concentrating on people who have received genuine contacts with extraterrestrial beings.

Having said that, the crop circle is undoubtedly an interesting phenomenon, and has been the focus for many books, seminars, websites, and media discussions. It really is a separate study from UFOs, although many try to link the two. This link is usually tenuous, to say the least, and films on YouTube and elsewhere that purport to show UFOs creating crop circles have to be viewed with caution. Just occasionally, though, a report comes along that cannot be disregarded. One of these was investigated by a friend of mine, UFO expert Ananda Sirisena. During a visit to Szolnok in Hungary to give a presentation about the planet Mars, Ananda met an elderly gentleman who had been researching UFOs and who told him that, before his retirement, he had worked in an electricity generating station from where UFOs had been sighted. On one occasion, they caused the power generation to fail when they appeared. He felt that the alien visitors wished to prevent some of the nuclear research that was being undertaken in that power station. He described to Ananda what happened when a team of maintenance men was attending to electricity pylons behind secure fences between 6 p.m. and 7 p.m. one evening. The men observed a light in the sky coming close to the pylon. It was a brightly illuminated object, which moved up and down the sky in a vertical line. He said they later discovered a crop circle exactly where the UFO had been hovering.

This anecdotal incident is echoed in certain other reports from other countries. Once, when I was doing a radio phone-in program in England's West Country, I received a call about a UFO sighting. The caller said that a crop circle appeared in a field over which the UFO had been seen too quickly for a fake circle of such complexity to be constructed. Experts in this subject, which I am not, say that there is a marked difference between the quality and sometimes beauty of a genuine crop circle, and one that has been created as a hoax. My view is that this is a subject about which we must keep a very open mind, but that it is not the main or best route to establishing contact with extraterrestrial civilizations.

I agree with Filipov that the use of radio signals is not the best way to make contact, either, and that telepathy is a far more effective and revealing method of communication with interplanetary races. They can already come here in their extraterrestrial spacecraft, if they wish to, and they clearly have a plan that determines the conditions and timing for open and direct contacts with the people of Earth as a whole. Just as they can control the degree to which they reveal themselves to us, so they could easily control, with their vastly superior technology, the radio-wave signals we can detect from them. In this case, the very costly program that SETI (Search for Extraterrestrial Intelligence) is engaged in seems futile. This US-based center has been mainly funded by donations from individuals and grants from private foundations, although it has received grants from NASA for some of its work. Its purpose is to discover evidence of life in the universe by looking for some sign of its technology. SETI uses radio telescopes, the idea being that just as radio-wave signals that originate from broadcasting stations, aircraft, and satellites can theoretically travel unlimited distances from Earth into space, so those that have been generated by distant civilizations could travel here. This would not be a case of making direct contact with them, but would demonstrate that they do exist.

If there was any doubt before whether contact with extraterrestrials was a government responsibility, we can now be sure that it is down to the ordinary citizen who is having extraordinary UFO experiences to determine the truth of this issue. There is no point in looking to officialdom for the answers, or even trying to find them by decoding crop circles. Insights come from those people who, much to their amazement, have had what became known in the 1970s as a close encounter of the third kind, i.e. physical contact with an extraterrestrial intelligence.

CHAPTER 4

A close encounter in Hampshire

Truth is always strange;
stranger than fiction.

Lord Byron

I n Oscar Wilde's inimitable words: "Whenever people agree with me, I always feel I must be wrong." Giordano Bruno, a Dominican monk, philosopher, astronomer, and mystic, was brave enough to go up against the accepted thinking of his day, saying, "Truth does not change because it is, or is not, believed by a majority of the people," but he paid the ultimate price for doing so and was burnt at the stake for heresy. That was in 1600 in Rome, and at the forefront of his ideals was a belief in the existence of life throughout the universe, which he said was infinite. He was almost a lone voice in a hostile climate, although the trail had been blazed by Nicholas of Cusa, a Catholic cardinal from Germany, in the fifteenth century, who had also speculated on life in the universe. In that earlier period, Nicholas of Cusa had somehow gotten away with it, but Bruno was not so fortunate. His ideas have been vindicated, though, and his "heretical" view is now held by a majority of people, including some within the Vatican.

In the 1970s, UFO witnesses were not threatened with the stake, but were up against a different kind of dogma. All kinds of so-called experts felt qualified to reason away UFO incidents, sometimes with explanations so far-fetched that they made the idea of extraterrestrial spacecraft seem conservative by comparison. Yet these debunkers were taken seriously at the time. In fact, there was an almost palpable sense of relief in some quarters that a seemingly qualified person had been able to dismiss the idea of alien beings visiting our world and so allow us all to get back to the safe normalities of everyday life.

The cigar-shaped object over Hull described in the Introduction, for example, which hundreds of people had witnessed, was very quickly explained away in the local media by a science professor from the university as being a barium cloud. This professor knew nothing about UFOs, and yet he felt that he was in a position to state authoritatively exactly what we had all seen. Modern research indicates that a barium cloud, even if it was to move slowly, would not hold the same shape for an extended period, nor would it be illuminated with a bright white light—and that assumes that conditions were right for it to form in the first place. However, a professor had said it was a barium cloud, and that was enough. People believed him, and this spectacular UFO sighting was conveniently shelved, leaving everyone who had seen it, or heard about it, free to go about their daily lives without being bothered by the need to question whether Hull had just played host to extraterrestrial visitors.

Being prepared to acknowledge that you don't know everything, certainly outside your area of expertise and even within it, is what I call the "Socrates test," and the professor completely failed it. Under questioning, Socrates is reputed to have described himself as the wisest man alive because he knew that he knew nothing. If that is an accurate quote, I consider it an inordinately bleak one—although that may well have been the whole point of it—but the lesson is worth remembering. Unfortunately, stating opinion as fact seems to have become acceptable, and these days you can see many so-called experts failing the test all the time. For example, historians will tell us with certainty exactly what made Henry VIII tick. They don't really know, they are just making an educated guess, perhaps an extremely educated guess, but still just a guess. That's fine if they know it's only a guess, but all too often they enter the dangerous sphere of thinking that they know beyond all doubt about the inner psychological motivations of an historical figure such as this. Fortified by the security of knowing that no one else is in a position to contradict them, they make their assertions boldly. Economists are renowned for expounding diametrically opposed theories, and yet they sometimes assert them as unalterable facts of economic law. They can't all be right—and based on recent financial developments globally, they might nearly all be wrong.

Back in the 1970s, when the doctrine that UFOs couldn't possibly exist held sway, some people seem to have been motivated by an almost fanatical determination to disprove the phenomenon at all costs. These are the ones who found some other explanation for a sighting, no matter how convincing the evidence. One of the most extreme cases of what could be categorized as "UFO denial syndrome" occurred after the "Kaikoura Lights" sightings over mountain ranges in the South Island of New Zealand in December 1978. At the time, I had just returned from a tour of New Zealand and Australia, where I had been giving talks and media interviews on UFOs, and I was therefore invited onto many radio shows in the UK to discuss these spectacular sightings. They began on December 21 when the crew of a cargo plane observed strange, lighted objects around their craft. The lights, some of them the size of a house, tracked them for several minutes, appearing on radar, and were witnessed by many people. On December 30 an Australian TV crew filmed a UFO event from on board a cargo aircraft flying between Wellington and Christchurch. One object followed the craft almost until landing. When the airplane took off again, an enormous orb-like object followed it for almost fifteen minutes. Again, the objects were tracked on radar, both from the airplane and by the air-traffic controler in Wellington, and many people saw them from the ground.

One of the early explanations given by the New Zealand government, which had conducted an investigation into these sightings, was that they were lights from the planet Venus. Even more amazingly, this was put out as a serious explanation in the media and many at the time unquestioningly believed it. Other explanations followed, including "flares from a Japanese squid fleet" and, a personal favorite of mine, "a flock of mutton birds coming inland to mate." At the speed they were traveling, those mutton birds must have been truly desperate!

Not all evidence is as convincing as the Kaikoura Lights, however, and it must be said, in the interests of balance, that some witnesses are quite capable of being carried away by their enthusiasm. The fact that a white light appears to move in the sky doesn't necessarily prove that it is an extraterrestrial spacecraft controlled by advanced beings. One type of UFO sighting you can be certain is an extraterrestrial spacecraft, however, is a close encounter of the third kind, when the witness usually sees the structure and shape of the craft and encounters one or more of those who man it. Such a witness was Joyce Bowles, whose experience in Hampshire, in the UK, was the subject of my first UFO investigation in November 1976. Also present at the encounter was a friend of hers, Ted Pratt. She was a very down-to-earth lady in her early forties, and he was a sensible man in his late fifties. Neither seemed the type of person to invent a cock-and-bull story, and they certainly had no incentive for doing so. All they received from most quarters for their candor and courage in coming forward with their experience was ridicule and contempt. I was one of the first to interview them, within days of the event taking place, and I found them convincing and credible witnesses. I have no reason to doubt that what they described occurred, and every reason to believe that it did.

The following is a verbatim transcription of my interviews with them, both conducted in their own homes, using a hand-held cassette tape recorder. Since its original publication in The Aetherius Society Newsletter in December 1976, this is the first time it has been reproduced in any other publication.

Mrs Joyce Bowles: At a quarter to nine in the evening on Sunday November 14th, I left my house to go and fetch my son, Stephen, who was at his girlfriend's place in Cheltenham. Mr Ted Pratt and his wife Rene came over for the day. On going at a quarter to nine, I asked Mr Pratt to come with me, and Rene to stay here to look after my younger children.

We got roughly a mile up the road, went round the large roundabout and down towards Winchester bypass and I caught a glimmer of an orange light, a large orange light, over my left-hand side. I said to Ted, "Look, Ted, look at that orange light!" He looked at it and then he said, "Mind, my girl, look where you're going," as I was the driver of the car. Then again I spotted the orange light, and I said, "Ted, just look at that—too late, mate, it's gone." The orange light was disappearing behind the back of some trees.

Going towards the bypass still, I had a sharp left-hand corner to turn round to go down Chilcomb Lane and into Chilcomb Village. I got down to second gear, went roughly five to six yards down the road when my car started shuddering and shaking. All of a sudden, the engine cut out, we were lifted off the road in our car and went sideways across this grass verge, which is rather large, near to a big hedge. We felt a slight bump in the car, which I gathered was when the car came to the ground. Then I saw this long cigar-shaped object. It had either white vapour or steam coming out from underneath. Inside this thing there were three people, but all we could see was their heads and shoulders. One of these people got out, although I never saw a door open, and he walked straight across. By the way, the cigar-shaped thing was at an angle to my car, and as he got out of this thing, he walked straight across to the window of my side of the car. While he was walking towards me, I heard a faint whistling, like a whistling kettle. Whether it was from this man or from the thing I don't know.

The man came to my window, put a hand on the roof of my car and bent down and looked in at Mr Pratt and myself. Firstly, he looked at me. He had large pink eyes. Then he looked at Mr Pratt. Afterwards he looked at the dashboard. As he looked at the dashboard, the engine of my car started up without the ignition key being turned on. And while the engine of the car started up, the bulbs of my car lights became four times the power of what they normally are. Incidentally, my car lights were on full beam, since I turned them on when I came off the bypass to go into the lane. I huddled into Mr Pratt, scared stiff. He wanted to get out of the car but I wouldn't let him. I just clung to him, and I opened one of my eyes, as I had shut them some of the time, and I said, "Look out, Ted, the man's going round the back of the car, he's going round your side." Ted looked over his left shoulder to wait for him to come round, while I clung to him with my eyes shut tight. Ted was looking on his left side, then all about, and he came to face me. He said, "I can't see nothing now, Joyce." We looked, and whatever it was, this thing, and this man, had gone.

Now the description of the man: he was six foot to six foot one tall. He had on something like a boiler suit with no reveres that had a high neck, like a round polo-neck. On the right-hand side he had what looked very much like a seam, but whether it was I don't know. His hair was shoulder length and turned up at the ends. He had a beard and sideburns, which came down to meet the beard.

After this gentleman went, Mr Pratt said, "Shall I drive your car, Joyce?" "Not likely," I said, only because I was scared to get out of my car. Mr Pratt said, "All right, Joyce, put her into first and see if she goes off." I switched the ignition on and put her into first gear to go off. I could not move. It was as though I was hitting against an invisible barrier and yet there was nothing whatsoever in front to stop the car. After I put her back in neutral, I waited for a while before I started the car up again and went off. The car has been going like a bomb ever since.

Richard Lawrence: Can you give any more description of the man? Of his face, would you say it was a kind face or anything like this?

JB: Mr Pratt unfortunately is the one who can give more detail of the man than I can. But as far as I know he wasn't an evil-looking man.

RL: The actual craft. You say it was cigar-shaped.

JB: What we could see of it was. It was like one of those fat cigars, shall we say like Sir Winston Churchill used to smoke, only bigger. This is the only way I can describe it. And it was glowing.

RL: How far away was it?

JB: About five yards.

RL: You have been contacted by many people since then. Roughly how many do you think?

JB: Oh, about three dozen.

RL: I believe you have been contacted by scientists who have investigated the case.

JB: Yes, but let's be truthful about this—what do they know about it?

RL: Could you mention any phone calls you have had?

JB: Yes, I had a phone call while a scientist was here at lunchtime today, telling me not to open my mouth about what I saw last Sunday—and that there would be a government official coming around to see me. I put the phone down, and then the scientist who was here went out immediately and made a phone call to London. He could not get hold of anyone he wanted to contact in London, so he phoned someone in Cosham I think. Then the phone rang again, within a matter of half an hour and it was the same gentleman. He warned me that on no account should I say anything about the incident at all and my remarks were, "This is not Russia, this is England, and I have a perfect right to say what I want, and what is the truth I will say."

RL: Did he give any reason why you shouldn't speak?

JB: No, he didn't. All he kept telling me was to shut my mouth.

RL: He didn't say what would happen if you did speak?

JB: He said harm could come to me, but he did not get the chance to say any more to me because I put the receiver back down.

RL: Have you had any other government investigation?

JB: No. I have had people here, but not from the government as far as I know, unless they are being cagey about it.

RL: I believe some people have tried to tell you that you didn't really see a flying saucer.

JB: Yes, that is perfectly true, and it makes me cross, because they come here trying to pick me to pieces, saying it was imagination or that it could have been a dairyman, or something. That is plain stupid. After all, if it had been a dairyman—and there is no dairy where I go to fetch my son—I would have known who it was, since I know all the dairymen in the area. But the same man who said that had also visited me on the Wednesday and said, "Mrs Bowles, I believe every word you say, because as I ask you questions, you do not hesitate, you look me straight in the face and answer me."

RL: And then he came back and told you it was a dairyman?

JB: He didn't actually straight out say he didn't believe me. When he came back today he was trying to find other excuses: "Oh, it could have been someone else, it could have been a dairyman." My remark to him was, "You people make me sick. You go to these colleges, and elsewhere, you read books, but you've never experienced anything yourself."

RL: Do you know where he came from?

JB: I'm not sure, but I think he comes from London.

RL: Apparently, he was concerned when you had these phone calls?

JB: Yes, he was very concerned.

RL: And it was after that that he mentioned the dairyman?

JB: After that he mentioned that it could have been a dairyman, or it could have been one of the big lights up on the new roundabout that we have at the top of the hill. And I said to him, "Look, Mr Wood, don't talk stupid. I know what I've seen and nothing else will convince me. Just because you have never seen it, don't start arguing with me."

RL: I believe somebody told you that these people would have wired you up, or something.

JB: Yes, that came from the gentleman who spoke to me over the phone.

RL: Oh, the same man as before?

JB: Yes.

RL: Did he frighten you?

JB: Yes, to be truthful he did frighten me at first—the way he was muttering on that telephone. He really got me convinced not to say anything to anyone.

RL: Because harm would come to you?

JB: Yes.

RL: Thank you very much, Mrs Bowles, for speaking so frankly to us.

JB: Well, it's the truth, and one can only speak the truth.

RL: What make is your car?

JB: It's a Mini Clubman Estate, and it was bought in July of this year.

RL: Have you had any trouble with it at all, since you bought it?

JB: No, none whatsoever.

RL: But during this particular incident it completely stopped?

JB: Yes, it cut out altogether. There is one little thing I would like to say though: that since the incident on Sunday, I don't have to use my choke half so much as I used to.

RL: So the car is actually in better condition now than it was before?

JB: Yes, it definitely is.

RL: Now, it lifted off the ground?

JB: Yes, definitely, all four wheels lifted off the ground. Mr Pratt caught hold of the steering wheel and tried to bring it down with a left-hand lock, hoping to straighten it out, but we could not do anything at all. There was something that took us over.

RL: Then, a few minutes later, you were back on the ground again?

JB: Then we came back down on the ground with a quiet bump, and that was when the craft, because I think that's what it was, appeared, and what I noticed first of all was the—either vapour or steam—that was coming out of the bottom of it. It was definitely five or six yards in front of me. Perhaps I am wrong in that. Mr Pratt could be more accurate than me. There is one other thing that I would like to say. People say, was it someone pretending or making it up? I'm sorry, I don't agree with people who say that. Mr Pratt suffers with angina, and yet he was cool and calm.

RL: Oh, he didn't show any fear throughout?

JB: He didn't show any fear throughout, and Mr Pratt feels that whatever that was gave him the power and the strength because of me. I was dead scared.

RL: You're not sure of the size of this craft, but you were able to see the whole craft, even though it was about five or six yards away?

JB: There could have been more of it than we saw, because it was glowing, you see. There is one thing that might be of interest to you. It was a nice moonlit night. Now, when this man was bent down looking in my car window, it was as though he was being blown up with a bicycle pump. His clothes were being blown out, like people on a windy day when they are riding a bicycle and their shirts blow out at the back. It could have come from a machine for all I know, but I am only describing to you what I saw.

RL: Yes, I believe you had a rash after this experience.

JB: Yes, on the right-hand side—that's where the gentleman came and looked in the window of my car. On Monday evening I had blotches all over my face, down the right side of my neck and along my shoulder. The blotches went off on Wednesday, and then all along my right shoulder it just literally burned, with just a little rash, as though somebody had put a red hot bottle on my shoulder. But today, it's a lot better, although it is still hot.

RL: It still feels hot now, does it?

JB: Yes, I wondered if perhaps it would have been nerves. But then surely nerves don't burn.

RL: No, it's hard to say. It doesn't sound like it was a road light, though.

JB: No, it wasn't, nor a dairyman. And anyone who says that—well, I feel like thumping them!

RL: So do I!

Ted Pratt: We left Mrs Bowles' house at about ten minutes to nine to go down to Chilcomb Farm to pick up her son Stephen, and while we were going down the bypass, we saw this very bright, reddy orange light in the sky. It came down very low and suddenly disappeared for a few seconds and then it suddenly appeared again to our left and then it disappeared again. We carried on down the Winchester bypass for roughly another quarter of a mile, then we turned left to get into Chilcomb Farm, which is a very narrow road—it's classed as a "B" road, I suppose. Well, we'd gone down there several yards. I estimate the speed at about 20 miles an hour, or maybe 25 miles an hour, and suddenly the car just, well, went mad. It just leaped off the road to the right for about two yards onto a very wide grass verge. It shuddered, it shook, and we were heading straight for a very high hedge. I leaned over, as Mrs Bowles was struggling with the steering wheel, and grasped the steering wheel with both my hands and tried to get a left-hand lock on but I couldn't move it.

RL: You were in the air then?

TP: No, we were not in the air then, we were on the ground and the car was shuddering and shaking and the engine was just racing at peak revs. Then diving down and racing up again. For all my efforts to pull the steering wheel round, nothing happened and then the car straightened itself. We went down along by this hedge for about ten to fifteen yards and then we came to a stop as though we had hit an invisible barrier. It was as though we had hit a rubber cushion, which gave to the impact and then brought us back again. The engine was still racing, so I switched it off but the headlights were absolutely brilliantly white, and in front of us was this deep orange glow, which I am going to call a space vessel, cigar-shaped. It was parked at a slight angle to the car. There was, I'm going to call it a windscreen as I've no other word to describe it, which curved around for quite a long way, and inside were three silhouettes of men—human beings. Inside was a light, but not brilliantly light—lemon color. It was quite clear in the control cabin, or control room, I should say.

RL: Could you actually see anything inside—machinery or gadgets or anything?

TP: No, I didn't see anything inside, except these three people. Then suddenly one man appeared through the side of this vehicle. I didn't see a door open, slide back or drop down or anything like that. I suddenly saw this man appear dressed in this silvery one-piece suit. My vision didn't register down below his knees and I didn't see what he had on his hands, but I did notice as he walked towards us, which took about four to five strides, that his face was absolutely deathly white, he had a beard, his hair was swept back up over his forehead down to his shoulders and then slightly curled up at the back. He approached the driver's side, where Mrs Bowles was sitting. He approached her window, looked at her and the most outstanding feature of him was his eyes, which—the complete eye, not the pupil, but the complete eyeball—were pink.

RL: Can you remember anything else about his face?

TP: His face was just a normal face: rather pointed nose; his mouth, his eyebrows were just exactly the same as any human being. Just an ordinary, placid face—he didn't look aggressive, but just a quiet looking man. In my estimation he was about six feet or just over six feet, slender built.

RL: What color was his hair?

TP: Rather—well, I can't call it blondish—it was a bit difficult to see with the brilliant glare of the space ship and the glare of our lights. I should say it was a light brownish in colour.

RL: Can you describe the craft in any more detail?

TP: The only way I can describe the craft is that it was cigar-shaped and from what I could see, there were four jets blowing out some kind of gases. It was hovering about eighteen inches off the ground. These gases, as they were blowing out, were just disappearing into the atmosphere.

RL: Like steam, or something like that?

TP: Yes, rather like steam. I estimated the length of the craft at about sixteen feet, and something between twelve and fourteen feet in height, but I couldn't say how wide the vessel was.

RL: What colour was the glow?

TP: Orange—very bright orange. This man, as I have said, approached the car window, looked in, and he looked at Mrs Bowles with his very, very piercing pink eyes, which seemed to terrify her, really petrify her. She just shook. She was petrified. Then he lifted his gaze and looked straight into my eyes, and I became very relaxed and very calm and my concern then was for her because she was so terrified. I looked down at her and tried to pacify her and I said, "Look, Joyce, I'm going to get out, I'm going to go round to him," and she said, "No." I think I said it about three times, "I'll get out and go round to him," but she was too terrified. His eyes left me and they roved along the dashboard of the car and the engine of the car started, and ran for several seconds, and then stopped. Then the man disappeared, and Mrs Bowles said, "I think he's going round to your side," so I glanced around the car, right round, but I couldn't see anything of him. So, I sat for a bit and I said, "Well, I think he's gone," because when I looked up, the bright orange glow of this vessel had disappeared also. I didn't hear it go. We sat there and I said, "Well, come along, we'll try and start and go." She said, "No, I'll drive," for the simple reason that she didn't want me to get out of that car. Well, she started the car and it started normally, she engaged low gear and gave it a few revolutions on the accelerator, but the car wouldn't go forward, it was hitting a barrier. It was some electrical ...

RL: Screen?

TP: Some electrical screen. We stood there, and the front wheels—because it was a Mini Clubman with a front wheel drive—spun. They tried to get a grip and just slipped, and the engine stalled. So we sat there for a few more seconds. I don't know how many seconds—I didn't even look at my watch. Then I said, "Come along, we'll try it again—come along, Joyce." We switched on the key and she started, she engaged gear again and just moved off normally and this vessel and the screen, or whatever it was, had gone. We drove off the grass onto the road—then went on down and picked up her son Stephen, who was waiting for us, and we turned round and I said to Stephen, "Stephen, what is the time?" He said, "It's two minutes past nine." I estimated the time we were stopped there with this vessel to be about five minutes.

RL: Would you say that this experience has changed you in any way?

TP: There are two things which amaze me. The first thing is that he wasn't wearing any head gear of any kind so he was breathing Earth atmosphere. Secondly, I suffer with angina. Did this person know that I suffer with angina? Was that why he looked at me so intensely and made me relax?

RL: Normally, an experience like that would have affected your health?

TP: Yes. That's why I'm at home. I have been at home now for four months, under the doctor, through this heart trouble. If he had really terrified me, that could have had disastrous results.

RL: So it's as if he generated some kind of power of a healing nature?

TP: Yes, he did indeed. I am sure he did.

RL: Now, I believe that ever since this incident you have had a feeling of mental relaxation or contentment.

TP: Yes, I have done.

RL: Do you feel as if you were given something?

TP: Yes, I do. I feel that I ought to have got out and gone round to this man and touched him. I feel that, because even just by visual contact, this relaxed feeling has come over me. I think by touching him—whether I'm right, whether I'm wrong, I don't see why they should do you any harm—I think if I had touched him, I think it might have done a lot more for me.

RL: So you really felt that here was someone who was only here to help?

TP: Yes, I did. If that man wanted to hurt us he could have literally torn that car to pieces. With their powers, which I know they must have got—they have got powers which we just don't know anything about, even our highest of scientists, I am positive about that—they could have torn that car to pieces and pulled us out of that car. But he wasn't on that mission. He was just on a peaceful mission to assure us that there was no harm in him at all.

RL: Did you believe in flying saucers before this?

TP: I believed in it. If they've sent people to the Moon, why can't somebody come down to us?

RL: But you wouldn't describe yourself as particularly interested in the subject before?

TP: Not before, but I am now. Definitely now. Yes.

It is laughable now to think that this encounter could be explained away with a straight face as being a milkman on an early morning round, and yet that idea was put about in the media and elsewhere and accepted by many. Apparently, this albino milkman with a very unusual milk truck and an extraordinary uniform was able to perform his early morning round on the previous evening at around 9 p.m. He also had healing powers and the ability to affect the car engine with a look. All one can say is that he was definitely in the wrong profession! This kind of explanation must sound so far-fetched as to be absurd, especially to younger readers, but the efforts to deny UFOs became more and more patently ludicrous. One believer told me that what had really convinced him more than anything else in the 1980s that UFOs existed was the absurd attempts to debunk them. Why, he wondered, would so much effort be made to deny this unless there was something in it—and something that really mattered?

To an open-minded person, Joyce and Ted's experience raises as many questions as it answers. Why would alien beings with technology such as that at their disposal select two Earth people on a quiet English road one evening to make their presence felt? Clearly, they were benign. Ted felt better for this encounter—if anything, his angina improved—and even the car ran better afterward. Why was it left to two ordinary people to try to convince others of what had happened to them, despite ridicule and even attempts to silence them? When I arrived to see her, Joyce told me that she had already been visited by someone who said he was called Richard Lawrence, and thinking it was me and knowing I was sympathetic to her claims, she had taken him into her confidence more than she would otherwise have done.

Why don't UFOs just land openly and prove themselves to everyone? Why pick an individual here, a couple there, a few people elsewhere, to make their presence felt? Why not all of us? If these aliens were hostile, they would have no concern for the effect they had on the mass of humanity. Fear, panic, mass hysteria would not matter to a cold, invading race. They would come regardless of how we felt about it. Clearly they are not hostile, and clearly they do take into account the reaction they receive. In this world of vested interests, political maneuvring, power games, and conflict, how would a mass landing by UFOs be received? There is no point in naively believing that our political leaders would defer to a race that was clearly more advanced in every respect than we are, or that the top financiers of the world would willingly relinquish their controlling tentacles of power, which infiltrate every aspect of world affairs.

And what if the message of our extraterrestrial visitors was not what people wanted to hear? What if their ideas weren't popular? What if they were not impressed by some of our entertainment and felt it should be curtailed? They might believe that we should be concerning ourselves with more important things than which celebrity is most popular in a jungle, or who is the best-dressed actor this year. And if so, would we want to change our behavior in the light of advice from a more advanced people?

There can be no doubt that all this and more would be known to such intelligences as these. They would factor it into their plan, and make their moves accordingly. When considering alien beings, it should not be from a standpoint of what we think they would do, but what they actually do. We might think an alien race would land openly and prove themselves to the whole world, but we are not them and they are by definition alien to us in their psychology as well as their habitat. All we can look at is what they do and have done for countless centuries—because they have been with us for all that time, as can be seen from the earliest writings that are still in existence.

CHAPTER 5

ETs in ancient records and religions

For then, before religion was despised,
the sky-dwellers in person used to visit
the stainless homes of heroes.

Catullus

T here was almost mutiny on deck among Christopher Columbus's small fleet, which had been at sea for over a month. The aim of the voyage was to discover land in a region where Columbus believed East Asia to lie, but no such land was in sight. Washington Irving, in his book *The Life and Voyages of Christopher Columbus*, first published in 1828, described the unfolding scenario:

They had already penetrated into seas untraversed by a sail, and where man had never before adventured. Were they to sail on until they perished, or until all return with their frail ships became impossible? Who would blame them, should they consult their safety and return? The admiral was a foreigner, a man without friends or influence. His scheme had been condemned by the learned as idle and visionary, and discountenanced by people of all ranks. There was, therefore, no party on his side, but rather a large number who would be gratified by his failure.

Such are some of the reasonings by which these men prepared themselves for open rebellion. Some even proposed, as an effectual mode of silencing all after complaints of the admiral, that they should throw him into the sea, and give out that he had fallen overboard, while contemplating the stars and signs of the heavens, with his astronomical instruments.

Columbus was not ignorant of these secret cabals, but he kept a serene and steady countenance, soothing some with gentle words, stimulating the pride or the avarice of others, and openly menacing the most refractory with punishment. New hopes diverted them for a time. On the 25th of September, Martin Alonzo Pinzon mounted on the stern of his vessel, and shouted, "Land! Land! Señor, I claim the reward?" There was, indeed, such an appearance of land in the southwest, that Columbus threw himself upon his knees, and returned thanks to God, and all the crews joined in chanting Gloria in excelsis. The ships altered their course, and stood all night to the southwest, but the morning light put an end to all their hopes as to a dream: the fancied land proved to be nothing but an evening cloud, and had vanished in the night.

On October 11 1492, history was about to be made. There were signs of land but nothing definite enough to convince Columbus, until a light appeared in the sky. Washington Irving continued the account:

He was now at open defiance with his crew, and his situation would have been desperate, but, fortunately, the manifestations of land on the following day were such as no longer to admit of doubt. A green fish, such as keeps about rocks, swam by the ships; and a branch of thorn, with berries on it, floated by; they picked up, also, a reed, a small board, and, above all, a staff artificially carved. All gloom and murmuring was now at an end, and throughout the day each one was on the watch for the long sought land.

In the evening, when, according to custom, the mariners had sung the *salve regina*, or vesper hymn to the virgin, Columbus made an impressive address to his crew, pointing out the goodness of God in thus conducting them by soft and favoring breezes across a tranquil ocean to the promised land. He expressed a strong confidence of making land that very night, and ordered that a vigilant lookout should be kept from the forecastle, promising to whomsoever should make the discovery, a doublet of velvet, in addition to the pension to be given by the sovereigns.

The breeze had been fresh all day, with more sea than usual; at sunset they stood again to the west, and were ploughing the waves at a rapid rate, the *Pinta* keeping the lead from her superior sailing. The greatest animation prevailed throughout the ships; not an eye was closed that night. As the evening darkened, Columbus took his station on the top of the castle or cabin on the high poop of his vessel. However he might carry a cheerful and confident countenance during the day, it was to him a time of the most painful anxiety; and now when he was wrapped from observation by the shades of night, he maintained an intense and unremitting watch, ranging his eye along the dusky horizon, in search of the most vague indications of land. Suddenly, about ten o'clock, he thought he beheld a light glimmering at a distance. Fearing that his eager hopes might deceive him, he called to Pedro Gutierrez, gentleman of the king's bedchamber, and demanded whether he saw a light in that direction; the latter replied in the affirmative. Columbus, yet doubtful whether it might not be some delusion of the fancy, called Rodrigo Sanchez of Segovia, and made the same inquiry. By the time the latter had ascended the round house, the light had disappeared. They saw it once or twice afterwards in sudden and passing gleams ...

On October 12, land was indeed sighted, which turned out to be San Salvador in the Bahamas. They had discovered what would become known as "The New World." The light that had appeared and disappeared in "sudden and passing gleams" was explained away as the torches of the indigenous residents of this island. Is that just another of those so-called explanations we are now so familiar with? Or could it have really been a far more important signal than that? Could it have been an extraterrestrial spacecraft, giving the final sign of encouragement on what was to become one of the most important voyages in history?

Such doubts still existed almost five hundred years later, on January 18 1979, when a historic debate took place in the House of Lords concerning UFOs and the existence of files about them held by the government, which had not at that stage been openly acknowledged. I was honored to be invited, since I was one of the speech writers for the Earl of Kimberley, who was a firm believer in this phenomenon, along with Ray Nielsen, who was then secretary of the European headquarters of The Aetherius Society. Seated as guests in the gallery overlooking the chamber, we witnessed this pivotal event, which would, in a subsequent debate, lead to a ministerial admission that these files did exist.

Among the contributions made by the Lords on that day, as reported in the House of Lords report in Hansard (the official report of the proceedings of the British Parliament), was one by the Bishop of Norwich, who called for a scientific investigation of this phenomenon. He said: "There was a time when leaders in the church were not always so enthusiastic about pushing out the frontiers of knowledge as I believe we are today. I very much hope that such a search will continue." He then quoted from the Epistle of Saint Paul to the Colossians in the New Testament, and went on: "I believe that Christ has not only a terrestrial, not only a cosmic significance, but literally a galactic significance—It is good that our minds and eyes should be stretched further out because I do not believe that at any point of the universe we get beyond the hand of God.

Therefore, it helps us to understand the majesty of the Godhead when we begin to stretch our minds to reach out to the far corners of creation."

At this point he was interrupted by one of his noble colleagues, Lord Trefgarne, who rose to ask: "Is he actually offering ecclesiastical authority for the existence of another race of people in another universe? Is he saying that the existence of UFOs, together with their inhabitants such as are so often described to us, is compatible with Christian faith?" The Bishop replied to Lord Trefgarne's question with the following reply: "I must say that I do not know—God may have other plans for other worlds, but I believe that God's plan for this world is Jesus. That at least is how I view the question." Despite his predictable endorsement of Christianity as the sole religion for this world, the Bishop's contribution to this debate did illustrate that the UFO phenomenon and the existence of extraterrestrials cannot be divorced from religion. Indeed, it is in the world religions that we often find the ancient records that reveal their long-term presence in our skies and, at times, among us.

Castel Gandolfo, a sixteenth-century monastery just south of Rome, houses the Vatican Observatory where four telescopes are kept along with the works of Copernicus, Galileo, Newton, Kepler, and others. The Vatican's meteorite museum is located there, too. Some researchers believe that the Vatican also has one of the largest UFO libraries in the world. Monsignor Corrado Balducci, who died in 2008, was a Catholic theologian and regarded as an insider close to the Pope. He openly postulated the likelihood of inhabited planets elsewhere. During a television interview in 1987 he speculated on the existence of beings with less material substance than ourselves who might well use UFOs. His views were echoed by Father José Gabriel Funes, an Argentinian Jesuit priest and astronomer, who became director of the Vatican Observatory in 2006 and, at the time of writing, is a scientific adviser to Pope Benedict. He stated that there was no contradiction between church teaching and the idea of intelligent extraterrestrials, making the interesting point that to rule out alien life would be to limit God's creativity.

If you were to strip away the church organization from Christianity, leaving only its core teachings, very few would argue that you would be left with one of the finest sets of values of all time—love for all people, forgiveness, tolerance, and service to others. You would be hard pushed to find much difference between this and the values at the root of all the great faiths in our world. The problems that arise in this and all religions can be the man-made constructs into which the fabric of these teachings is woven. Foremost among these, as far as the traditional churches are concerned, is the concept of the trinity. This was articulated at the turn of the fourth century CE by Saint Augustine, undoubtedly with the best of intentions, in order to remove the differences of interpretation, which had already been rife for hundreds of years in the early Christian church. But then they do say that the road to hell is paved with good intentions.

During the early period of Christianity, some believed that Jesus was a great prophet, others that he was God incarnate. Many people fell somewhere between these two polarized views. Saint Augustine and others—some of whom had a questionable, politicized motive in the early ecumenical councils—standardized these different views with the concept of the trinity. This doctrine became universally adopted throughout the church and the incontrovertible dogma developed that God had decided to appear in human form and to die after a life of thirty-three years in order to save us from our sins. He did this once and only once in the entire history of the human race, choosing the middle-eastern region of this world in which to live and to teach a relative handful of people before returning from whence he came. This concept may not sound strange to you—indeed, it may be something you believe to be true—but I suggest that, from a global theological point of view, it is an absolutely extraordinary explanation for what really happened.

Another possible explanation would be as follows. The Master Jesus was an exceptionally elevated being from the planet Venus ("the bright and morning star" referred to in Revelations, chapter 22, verse 16), who came to Earth in an extraterrestrial spacecraft in order to live among us. His main mission here was to die in order to bear karma on behalf of the human race. He was not, and could not be, tricked by Judas, but deliberately arranged to die in the way that he did, after which he rose from the dead as had been demonstrated by others before him on rare occasions, especially in the East. He also delivered one of the most profound, spiritual sets of teachings ever given to Earth, which has been modified in the hands of religious leaders and translators.

My point here is not to convert or to convince you of the second explanation, even though I believe it to be true. It would take serious investigation and contemplation before accepting either conclusion. But I suggest that, of the two, it is the more likely to an impartial observer. If it doesn't seem so, that is only because of its relative unfamiliarity. We are used to the idea of Jesus being the one and only Son of God. It is an idea that has permeated the thinking of the world for many hundreds of years, and therefore does not seem strange. I contend that if someone who had never heard of Jesus before, or the theological ideas of the church, was presented with those two options, they would find the first one much more difficult to accept.

My own view is that UFOs and the existence of extraterrestrial beings provide the missing link in religion. There is not a one and only way, but a variety of paths presented in different ways at different times in human history, to achieve the same goal of oneness with God. Many of these teachings, in my view, were instigated by beings from other worlds and brought to this Earth, either by one or more of their number, or by those who were in direct contact with them. Hence the religious traditions of our world, and the ancient records from which they are sourced, provide one of the richest veins in which to mine the truth about our cosmic visitors.

The motivating principle that governs these elevated travelers from space seems not to be technology, but cooperation with the divine laws, which have been expressed in numerous ways throughout our history. Mistakenly, we have tended to think that if you are a Buddhist, you are not a Christian, or if you are a Hindu, you cannot be a Jew. On the contrary, some of the texts of Buddhism and Christianity are remarkably similar, and an ancient Sanskrit mantra is very close in meaning, when translated, to the name of the God of the Old Testament, which is referred to as "I Am That I Am." Those who created these religious paths were directed by the same extraterrestrial intelligences and were playing their parts in the same cosmic plan.

Ancient records and legends about UFOs have been with us for thousands of years. The earliest writings are, for the most part, religious texts. These were sometimes the product of centuries of oral tradition before ever being put down in writing, and it is as though the religious teachings of the world are being looked at through an out-of-focus telescope. As soon as UFOs and cosmic existence are brought into the picture, the focus improves and their real meaning becomes ever clearer. UFOs do not lessen our appreciation of God's creation, they enhance it. They fill in the gaps. Without a cosmic concept within religious teachings, numerous unanswered questions hang in the air, such as: Is Jesus the one and only Son of God in the system of Alpha Centauri? Do cosmic beings enter nirvana throughout the Milky Way? Have the Ten Commandments been delivered to other planetary races? Sooner or later, the Pope, the Dalai Lama, the Chief Rabbi, and other religious leaders will have to address the issue of how interplanetary existence impinges upon their faiths. It need not lessen them and it cannot be ignored forever.

The major religious texts are packed with incidents and descriptions of UFOs, connected with some of the greatest religious figures in our history—Moses, Rama, and Jesus to name but three.

Here is an example from an ancient holy work of the Hindu faith, *The Mahabharata*, translated by Roy Pratap Chandra more than a hundred years ago:

> **Causing the heaven and the earth to be filled by a loud sound**, then Indra came to Yudhishthira on a car [vimana] and asked him to ascend it. Seeing his brothers fallen on the earth, King Yudhishthira the just said to that deity of a thousand eyes these words: "My brothers have all dropped down here! They must go with me. Without them by me, I do not wish to go to the celestial region, O lord of all the celestials. The delicate princess Draupadi, deserving of every comfort, should go with us! You should permit this."
>
> Indra answered, "You shall behold your brothers in the celestial region. They have reached it before you. Indeed, you shall see all of them there, with Krishna. Do not give way to grief, O chief of the Bharatas! Having renounced their human bodies they have gone there, O chief of the Bharata race! As for you, it is ordained that you shall go there in this very body of yours ..."
>
> Then Dharma and Indra and the other deities, causing Yudhishthira to ascend on a car, went to the celestial region. Those beings crowned with success and capable of going everywhere at will, rode their respective cars. King Yudhishthira, riding on his car, ascended quickly, causing the entire sky to blaze with his effulgence.

The key Sanskrit word for UFO enthusiasts in this text is "vimana." The internet is full of references to vimanas because they are evidence of the long-term presence of extraterrestrial visitors in our skies. Translated variously as flying vehicle, aerial chariot, or airborne car, vimana is a better term than UFO or the very twentieth-century flying saucer. In the passage quoted above, for example, Chandra uses the word "car," which is not surprising considering the period in which he translated it. These texts make it clear that vimanas are very much identified flying objects, and that they are superb aircraft of great beauty, speed, and versatility. There is even reference to vimanas having the capacity to become invisible, something that thousands of UFO spotters have witnessed when these objects disappear and reappear. Gods, such as Rama and other elevated beings, travel in these vimanas, sometimes meeting with other enlightened or more prominent intelligences than themselves. In this extract, for example, there is reference to Sri Krishna being in the celestial region. Taken literally, this could imply that Sri Krishna, who delivered one of the most profound of all ancient teachings, *The Bhagavad Gita*, was himself an extraterrestrial being. What better explanation could there be than this for his otherworldly wisdom and powers?

Just how old sacred Hindu works are is open to debate. Some scholars say that certain of them are at least five thousand years old, and others could be far more ancient even than this, because the texts, or Vedas, were said to have been handed down orally for many generations among those who had the ability to memorize long passages of scripture and had no need of the written word. In the light of this, some believe that the Vedas describe events that occurred tens or even hundreds of thousands of years ago.

Mention is made in this extract from *The Mahabharata* of King Yudhishthira having discourse with a deity—which occurs frequently in the Bible, for example in relation to Moses. This deity is referred to as "lord of all the celestials," which suggests he is a prominent interplanetary being. The term could be equated to Cosmic Master, which can be used to describe an advanced spiritual being from another world. Reference to "brothers in the celestial region" also suggests that these beings are from other worlds. The text then becomes more mystical and seems to have an affinity with some of the teachings found in theosophy, Rosicrucianism, and elsewhere. The king's brothers have renounced their physical bodies and traveled to the celestial region, indicating an out-of-body experience in which the psycho-spiritual aspect of our being travels independently of the human form. Gurus and mystics have claimed to be able to travel through space in their astral bodies and even to visit other worlds, as will be described more fully in later chapters. Nevertheless, the king is required to remain in his physical body to travel in the vimana and, with the help of the celestial deities, this is what he does. The deities, we are told, are capable of going everywhere at will, a theme that recurs in Sanskrit writings in relation to vimanas. This suggests that an element of mental control is necessary in relation to these spacecraft.

Danger lies in taking such accounts too literally, and I don't believe that the Hindu Vedic texts, or indeed the Bible, can be regarded as entirely accurate. However, they do provide the best accounts we have of some of the most important events in our ancient history, and they certainly should not be ignored. Where a pattern of consistent references to happenings emerges, you should surely take notice of it, and there is one in respect of UFOs and their spiritual connections.

Throughout the Bible, reports of aerial phenomena are to be found—stories spanning thousands of years abound with evidence of UFOs. Descriptions vary from calling them clouds to referring to them as moving objects, glowing brightly, often with a fiery appearance. For example, the Book of Ezekiel, chapter 1, verse 4, says (all quotations used here come from the King James version of the Bible):

> And I looked, and, behold, a whirlwind came out of the north, a great cloud, and a fire infolding itself, and a brightness was about it, and out of the midst thereof as the colour of amber, out of the midst of the fire.

In verse 16, the description of the UFO becomes more detailed:

> The appearance of the wheels and their work was like unto the colour of a beryl: and they four had one likeness: and their appearance and their work was as it were a wheel in the middle of a wheel.

An account of the departure of Elijah, who was taken up into the sky, never to be seen again physically, appears in 2 Kings, chapter 2, verse 11. Elijah was talking with his successor, Elisha:

> And it came to pass, as they still went on, and talked, that, behold, there appeared a chariot of fire, and horses of fire, and parted them both asunder; and Elijah went up by a whirlwind into heaven.

Many theories about what actually helped Moses to lead his people out of Egypt have been put forward. Some of these have speculated that the intervention of extraterrestrial spacecraft enabled the exodus to take place, and in biblical accounts, pillars and clouds certainly appear to have protected and guided the people of Israel to a safe and fertile land. The Book of Exodus, chapter 13, verse 21 says:

> And the LORD went before them by day in a pillar of a cloud, to lead them the way; and by night in a pillar of fire, to give them light; to go by day and night:

Chapter 14, verses 19-20 seem to suggest direct intervention to prevent the Israelites being attacked by the Egyptians:

19　And the angel of God which went before the camp of Israel, removed, and went behind them; and the pillar of the cloud went from before their face, and stood behind them:

20　And it came between the camp of the Egyptians and the camp of Israel; and it was a cloud and darkness to them, but it gave light by night to these: so that the one came not near the other all the night.

One could infer that the Ten Commandments themselves were delivered by a being from another world, who traveled in a UFO. The Book of Exodus, chapter 34, verses 1-5, states:

1　And the LORD said unto Moses, Hew thee two tables of stone like unto the first: and I will write upon these tables the words that were in the first tables, which thou brakest.

2　And be ready in the morning, and come up in the morning unto mount Sinai, and present thyself there to me in the top of the mount.

3　And no man shall come up with thee, neither let any man be seen throughout all the mount; neither let the flocks nor herds feed before that mount.

4　And he hewed two tables of stone like unto the first; and Moses rose up early in the morning, and went up unto mount Sinai, as the LORD had commanded him, and took in his hand the two tables of stone.

5　And the LORD descended in the cloud, and stood with him there, and proclaimed the name of the LORD.

These events happened some time after the Ten Commandments were delivered to Moses on Mount Sinai by the Lord. He went back up the mountain with the two tables of stone to have the commandments inscribed on them, and the Lord, descending in a cloud, proceeded to give further instructions. In my view, this was a cosmic being coming at a critical time in our history to give vital guidance and teaching. The Ten Commandments were, after all, to become the bedrock of western morality—although, arguably, they have not yet been put into practice particularly well!

What are these clouds that appear on several occasions in the Old and New Testaments, behaving as no cloud should? Perhaps they could have been more accurately described as unidentified, or even identified, flying objects. Take the following passage for example. By this stage, the tabernacle containing the Ark of the Covenant is being transported toward the promised land, and it seems that at every stage the travelers are guided by the presence of a cloud, which even directs them when to rest and when to move. This detailed extract sounds a bit like the plot of a Steven Spielberg film—"Indiana Jones" meets "Close Encounters of the Third Kind." It is taken from the Book of Numbers, chapter 9, verses 17–23:

17 And when the cloud was taken up from the tabernacle, then after that the children of Israel journeyed: and in the place where the cloud abode, there the children of Israel pitched their tents.

18 At the commandment of the LORD the children of Israel journeyed, and at the commandment of the LORD they pitched: as long as the cloud abode upon the tabernacle they rested in their tents.

19 And when the cloud tarried long upon the tabernacle many days, then the children of Israel kept the charge of the LORD, and journeyed not.

20 And so it was, when the cloud was a few days upon the tabernacle; according to the commandment of the LORD they abode in their tents, and according to the commandment of the LORD they journeyed.

21 And so it was, when the cloud abode from even unto the morning, and that the cloud was taken up in the morning, then they journeyed: whether it was by day or by night that the cloud was taken up, they journeyed.

22 Or whether it were two days, or a month, or a year, that the cloud tarried upon the tabernacle, remaining thereon, the children of Israel abode in their tents, and journeyed not: but when it was taken up, they journeyed.

23 At the commandment of the LORD they rested in the tents, and at the commandment of the LORD they journeyed: they kept the charge of the LORD, at the commandment of the LORD by the hand of Moses.

These are just some of the many extracts that I could have chosen in which clouds with very unusual properties are referred to during the exodus of the Israelites from Egypt to the promised land. They are regularly seen following, or even, by implication, guiding, Moses and his followers as they made their precarious journey to safety. Was this because it was deemed essential by the Cosmic Masters that a religion adhering to the concept of one God deserved protection at that time? The scribes who compiled the Bible did not understand the formation of clouds, nor were they familiar with the idea of space travel. They could only describe what it looked like—a moving, white body in the sky, something like a cloud, in fact.

The disciples of Jesus, too, witnessed divine intervention in the form of a cloud, after receiving instructions from the resurrected Jesus. In Acts, chapter 1, verses 9–11, the text reads as follows:

9   And when he had spoken these things, while they beheld, he was taken up; and a cloud received him out of their sight.

10 And while they looked stedfastly toward heaven as he went up, behold, two men stood by them in white apparel;

11 Which also said, Ye men of Galilee, why stand ye gazing up into heaven? this same Jesus, which is taken up from you into heaven, shall so come in like manner as ye have seen him go into heaven.

This prophecy that Jesus would return in a cloud also occurs in Matthew, chapter 24, verse 30:

And then shall appear the sign of the Son of man in heaven: and then shall all the tribes of the earth mourn, and they shall see the Son of man coming in the clouds of heaven with power and great glory.

Another fascinating example of the interaction between Jesus, his disciples, and a cloud is to be found in Mark, chapter 9, verses 2–8:

2   And after six days Jesus taketh with him Peter, and James, and John, and leadeth them up into an high mountain apart by themselves: and he was transfigured before them.

3 And his raiment became shining, exceeding white as snow; so as no fuller on earth can white them.
4 And there appeared unto them Elias with Moses: and they were talking with Jesus.
5 And Peter answered and said to Jesus, Master, it is good for us to be here: and let us make three tabernacles; one for thee, and one for Moses, and one for Elias.
6 For he wist not what to say: for they were sore afraid.
7 And there was a cloud that overshadowed them: and a voice came out of the cloud, saying, This is my beloved Son: hear him.
8 And suddenly, when they had looked round about, they saw no man any more, save Jesus only with themselves.

This fascinating account of an interaction between Jesus, Elias (Elijah), and Moses suggests their otherworldly origin. The voice coming out of a cloud is possibly somewhat reminiscent of the audio system described by Dan Fry (see Chapter 2) although clearly in a far more elevated context.

However, perhaps the most explicit statement is made in John, chapter 17, verse 16, when Jesus says of his disciples:

They are not of the world, even as I am not of the world.

There were records of cosmic visitors in the Middle East in the region of Mesopotamia even before the Bible. From there comes the so-called Sumerian king list, which is an ancient manuscript in the Sumerian language, listing kings from Sumerian and foreign dynasties. It records their locations together with the rulers and the length of their reigns. Significantly, the Sumerians believed that these kingships were originally bequeathed by the gods and were transferable between cities. Prehistoric, exceptionally lengthy reigns give way to later historical dynasties of more conventional length. Some historians regard the predynastic kings as a work of fiction, but they are given the same legitimacy in existing records as are the later known rulers. Incidentally, at least one of the rulers was female.

If taken literally, the Sumerian king list dates back hundreds of thousands of years, with early reigns stretching over tens of thousands of years, and the rulers being regarded as gods, demi-gods, or immortals. Sumerian clay tablets and cylinder seals support the king list. Among the early gods were the Anunnaki, who were believed to have descended from the sky to the Earth. According to some sources, they were believed to have come from a planet called Nibiru. One year on Nibiru was said to be the equivalent of three thousand Earth years, which, in itself, is a very interesting concept from a mystical point of view. The Sumerians may also have believed that the Anunnaki brought new technologies and great wisdom about our place in the solar system. All of this is dismissed by some people as pure mythology without historical foundation.

The Assyrians and Babylonians are said to have believed that their chief god, Marduk, came from another planet. According to the Babylonian creation myth, Marduk assigned the Anunnaki to their various stations in heaven and on Earth. These earliest of legends from the Middle East, however one interprets them, signify a belief in greater beings coming to our world from other planets.

In the Far East, evidence of UFO activity and extraterrestrials is said to pre-date even Sumerian civilization. On an island in Hunan province in China, granite carvings depict what some researchers have taken to be extraterrestrial spacecraft, cylindrical in shape, possibly with an alien crew inside. These have been dated to some 47,000 years ago—during the era of Neanderthal man.

Another fascinating discovery came to light in the mountainous region on the borders of Tibet. A team of archaeologists carrying out a routine survey in 1938 stumbled on a large round stone disk, etched with hieroglyphs. For twenty years, experts in Beijing tried to translate the markings until, finally, Professor Tsum Um Nui claimed to have broken the code. Several years later, in 1965, according to reports, another professor, Dr Chi Pu Tei, and his team of four colleagues were given permission to publish their theory of the hieroglyphs' meaning, under the title "The grooved script concerning spaceships which as recorded on the discs landed on Earth 12,000 years ago." More than seven hundred disks had been uncovered, apparently revealing that a space probe had been conducted by beings from another world in the mountain range of Bayan-kara-ula. They told how the peaceful intentions of these aliens had been misunderstood by the hostile inhabitants of the Ham tribe, who lived in the region. The hieroglyphs were interpreted as describing these beings traveling in aircraft. One spaceship had allegedly crash-landed, like some prehistoric version of the Roswell incident. The extraterrestrial visitors were described as having huge heads and weak bodies.

The mystery does not end there. Several of the disks were later sent to Moscow for examination by Russian scientists, who put them through chemical analysis. They detected large amounts of cobalt and other metallic substances, and the disks, when placed on a turntable, vibrated in an unusual rhythm as though an electrical charge was passing through them. Dr Vyatcheslav Saizev described these amazing findings in the Soviet magazine *Sputnik*. One scientist suggested that the disks were part of some electrical circuit, indicating that at some time in the past they had been exposed to extraordinarily high voltages. Could this fact point to some otherworldly technology at work?

The Dogon people, who live in the rocky hills, mountains, and plateaus of the Bandiagara Escarpment of Mali in Western Africa, also believe they received their knowledge from extraterrestrial visitors. They say that these beings came from Sirius some three thousand years ago. A ceremony, called the *sigui*, is performed every sixty years when the star Sirius appears between two mountain peaks. French anthropologist Marcel Griaule had been studying the Dogon tribe for some sixteen years when, in the 1940s, he was initiated into the secret knowledge of the Dogon elders. This had been passed down orally to the select few within their community for centuries. Among other things, they told him about the rings of Saturn, the moons of Jupiter, the Milky Way being a spiral galaxy of stars, and the fact that the planets of this solar system move in orbits around the Sun.

They revealed to Griaule their special reverence for Sirius, and their belief that it comprised three stars even when only one star, Sirius A, had been identified, and they also specified that the second of these stars, Sirius B, was invisible and extremely heavy. American astronomer Alvan Clark had discovered Sirius B in 1862, and it turned out to be a white dwarf, and therefore of such dense matter as to be exceedingly heavy. The authenticity of some of these claims is disputed, but the Dogons have been the subject of intensive investigation and seem to know things that were not accessible to European astronomers at the time, never mind to a tribe in a remote part of Africa. The alleged third Sirius star is yet to be discovered. Some astronomers have proposed that certain perturbations in that system could be explained by the existence of a small red dwarf star, which would then be Sirius C.

According to the late Lord Clancarty, who wrote under the name Brinsley Le Poer Trench, an Egyptian papyrus exists from the reign of Thutmos III in the fifteenth century BC, which describes a series of UFO sightings. The first mentions a circle of fire, suggesting the classic disk-shape described in modern times as a flying saucer. According to this papyrus, a few days later the skies were filled with these fire circles, which were seen by the pharaoh and his army after supper one evening.

Over a thousand years later, in 329 BCE, the most powerful ruler on Earth at that time, Alexander the Great, saw shining, shield-like objects flying above him and his army as they attempted to overcome the opposition and cross the river Indus. These gleaming, silver objects swooped down and made several passes over the battle, startling his cavalry horses and causing them to stampede. Allegedly as a result, Alexander decided to proceed no farther into India. Was this their purpose for being there? Maybe this was one region in which, for some reason best known to our cosmic visitors, imperialism and the indoctrination of Greek culture could not be allowed. Was this just one step too far for the conqueror to take? Maybe his other military ventures were looked upon with disapproving eyes by these beings, but could it be that a move by Alexander the Great into India could not be permitted? Perhaps it was because the wisdom that already existed there was greater than the philosophy and learning Alexander wanted to introduce through conquest, and therefore this region was not to be tampered with.

Very old Japanese documents describe an unusual shining object seen on the night of October 27 1180, which was heading northeast toward a mountain in Kii Province. It suddenly changed direction and vanished, leaving a trail of light in its wake. The phrase used to describe this sighting was "flying earthenware vessel." So perhaps UFOs being designated as airborne crockery is not exclusive to the twentieth century after all!

Europe, too, is full of records that could be taken to indicate UFO activity, from the ancient classical period through to the present day. One example appears in the work of Conrad Lycosthenes, a sixteenth-century professor of grammar and dialectics from Alsace. In his work *Prodigiorum ac Ostentorum Chronicon* he describes how strange lights were seen in the sky during the reign of Emperor Theodosius in AD 393. He states that a bright glow appeared near Venus, following which several other orbs, rather like a swarm of bees, appeared around it. They all blended together to form what seemed to be a two-edged sword in the sky. Also in this book, which is kept in the research library of the Australian Museum, is a depiction of a cylindrically shaped UFO in Arabia in 1479. Cylinder and disk are the two shapes most often attributed to UFOs in history. Zechariah, for example, in the Old Testament, describes the sighting of a "flying roll," by which he means a rolled-up manuscript (not a moving snack!). This type of UFO would, in more recent times, be referred to as cigar-shaped.

Pictures from European galleries and archives provide a rich source of UFO documentation. They absolutely disprove the notion that this is some kind of new phenomenon, first illustrated in the twentieth century. We have to understand, though, that compilers of records before man-made flying craft were invented have a very different way of illustrating this phenomenon. Intelligently directed clouds were not unique to the Bible. On August 18 1783, at 9.45 p.m., four witnesses on the terrace of Windsor Castle in Berkshire, England, observed a luminous object in the sky. This was recorded in 1784 in *Philosophical Transactions of the Royal Society*. It describes what these witnesses saw:

> **An oblong cloud moving more or less parallel to the horizon**. Under this cloud could be seen a luminous object which soon became spherical, brilliantly lit, which came to a halt; this strange sphere seemed at first to be pale blue in colour, but then its luminosity increased and soon it set off again towards the east. Then the object changed direction and moved parallel to the horizon before disappearing towards the southeast; the light it gave out was prodigious; it lit up everything on the ground.

One of the witnesses that night was Thomas Sandby, a founding member of Britain's Royal Academy, who captured it for posterity in one of his illustrations.

Astronomers estimate that there are ten billion trillion stars in the known universe. Many of these stars have planets orbiting around them, as we are continuing to discover, so the idea of space-traveling aliens is virtually a given. To the medieval Christian, the Earth was the center of the universe, and the exact nature of planets was unknown. Although there was a widely held belief in angels, no notion of the technology connected with space travel existed, or any idea that angels would require vehicles to make their cosmic journeys. Despite this, some of the depictions in the artistic masterpieces of the Middle Ages and the Renaissance are startling in their consistency with modern UFO reports.

"The Madonna with Saint Giovannino," painted by Domenico Ghirlandaio in the fifteenth century, shows an object above Mother Mary's left shoulder that is clearly disk-shaped, not too dissimilar to the photograph taken by George Adamski. A man and his dog can be seen in the background, looking up at this object. At the National Gallery in London, "The Annunciation with

Saint Emidius" by Carlo Crivelli shows a disk-shaped object in the sky. Frescoes and tapestries show flying objects, and sometimes beings within them. From Kosovo to Beaune to Florence, churches and monasteries contain illustrations of what are clearly flying objects connected to religious scenes. In the Academy of Florence, a painting by Paolo Uccello entitled "La Tebaide" shows a red saucer-shaped UFO near Jesus at the moment of his crucifixion.

Sometimes these depictions in European art are almost journalistic in their approach. One such is a picture of a UFO sighting over Basle in Switzerland in 1566, which is held at the Zurich Central Library. I could go on and on with examples, many of which can be found on the internet. However, one staggering picture of a classic UFO that must be mentioned is "The Baptism of Christ," painted by Flemish artist Aert de Gelder in 1710. It currently hangs in the Fitzwilliam Museum in Cambridge, England. This shows John the Baptist baptizing the Master Jesus in an aura of golden light, with a beautiful disk-shaped spacecraft hovering over the scene.

To document the numerous sightings described in European writings from the medieval period onward would be superfluous and somewhat dull. Such records can easily be found by anyone who is interested, showing how monks and other scribes witnessed objects looking like pillars, small boats, revolving wheels, cylinders, and so forth, flying through the skies. One thing that is absolutely certain is that this phenomenon has been with us through the centuries. It has been documented in writing and pictorial form for as long as our records exist.

The claims are so broad and all-encompassing that only someone determined not to believe in UFOs could really dismiss them. An example of this occurred while I was in the process of writing this book. An article appeared in a London newspaper, describing how a retired man had a close encounter of the third kind while walking his dog in a park in the West Country. He reportedly saw a round object about thirty feet in diameter and a hundred feet long, with blue and red flashing lights on its perimeter, land in the park. A four-foot translucent, white shape apparently moved toward him and his dog, which started to growl. The apparition was described as making a droning noise, which transfixed the man. The report said that he was terrified and ran away as soon as he could. For me, even more disappointing than his fear, which many would understand, was that he reportedly remained a skeptic even after this outstanding experience.

Whether the man in this report was an outright disbeliever or just had some doubts about it, there really are people who would not believe in a UFO if it landed in their garden and an alien being entered their house and stood in front of them. They would find some kind of psychological explanation, such as hallucination, to dismiss even a cast-iron experience of their own. It was the French thinker Voltaire who said: "Earth is an insane asylum, to which the other planets deport their lunatics." In one sense, he could not have been more wrong—our extraterrestrial visitors have been the wisest and most evolved intelligences ever to walk the Earth—but the spirit of his humorous quip is absolutely right, for it is the behavior of humans, not that of our cosmic visitors, that is psychologically questionable.

Extraterrestrial beings have undoubtedly featured throughout many ancient records and religious traditions in one way or another, and this chapter can only touch on a selection of particularly significant examples of them. They are said to be depicted in the cave drawings of the aborigines. Joseph Smith, founder of Mormonism in America in the 1820s, claimed that he learned from the Angel Moroni that many inhabited worlds exist in the cosmos. The great Hindu saint, Sri Ramakrishna, who lived in India in the latter part of the nineteenth century, had several disciples, the most prominent and well known of whom was the great Swami Vivekananda. Another of his disciples was Swami Yogananda, who should not be confused with Paramahansa Yogananda, author of the beautiful *Autobiography of a Yogi*. The Swami Yogananda, who followed Sri Ramakrishna, was described as being calm, mild, and sweet of nature. Since early boyhood, he had believed that he was not of this world but from a distant group of stars where his companions remained. Whether this is true is open to speculation, but he was certainly a highly respected and accomplished spiritual devotee.

Perhaps, of all the traditional religions, extraterrestrial life is best explained in Buddhist teachings. Ananda Sirisena has conducted a study of this subject and come up with the following very interesting findings, which he shared with me for this book. The Lord Buddha clearly stated that he came from another world and that he had met otherworldly beings while he was on Earth 2,500 years ago. In the Buddhist scripture *Digha Nikaya* a story is recounted that the Buddha gave teaching to an intelligence from beyond this Earth, who had become mentally deluded and had assumed mighty powers. Through this teaching, the delusion was corrected.

The Lord Buddha taught that life is prevalent throughout the universe, manifesting in different spheres of existence and levels of consciousness, which he referred to as "lokas." He stated that two-footed, four-footed, no-footed, and many-footed beings existed throughout the universe. It seems that he had a very open and broadminded view of extraterrestrial civilizations. In the *Ang Uttara Nikaya* (*The Book of Tens*), the Lord Buddha describes a time when beings will be reborn in the heaven of radiant deities. There they will live joyous and glorious lives, radiating light and traversing the skies for a long time until further transformation takes place. Buddhism links the many levels or spheres of existence to states of consciousness, and makes reference to spontaneously mind-born beings, implying that there are higher evolutionary realms of existence beyond this world, where procreation is not necessary. There have been occasional claims of virgin births in our history, the most famous being that of Jesus, but a spontaneous mind-created birth implies that even this would not be necessary, i.e. the whole physical process would be redundant.

Buddhism makes little distinction between the concept of life on other planets and life on other planes, concentrating on a universe of lokas delineating different degrees of spiritual evolution. For example, one level is the world of great Brahma, meaning beings more evolved than humanity. There are worlds of Brahma of minor luster, infinite luster, minor aura, infinite aura, and steady aura. There are worlds of creatively rewarded, sensationalist, serene, beautiful, clear-sighted, and supreme Brahma. The highest of all the thirty-one spheres or levels of consciousness is beyond the senses or mental perception and is linked to the concept of nirvana. Buddhist texts teach that the life span in some of these worlds is aeons—so long as to be incalculable—and that communication with those on higher spheres and from other worlds is possible for those who have attained the most profound levels of meditation.

A significant reference in the *Tevijja Sutta* mentions the Lord Buddha giving some intimation of his knowledge of other worlds. When asked whether he knew the path to higher Brahma, he answered that he knew it as one who has entered those worlds and been born within them. The Lord Buddha was known as a teacher of gods and men, who spoke about the plurality of gods throughout the universe and the varying abodes, planes, and levels of consciousness throughout the cosmos.

This concept of lokas is not a million miles from ground-breaking scientific research that is taking place now. The awesome possibilities of a cosmic landscape, teeming with life in the physical world as we know it and also in other dimensions, are preoccupying the minds of some of our most forward-thinking scientists. It is fascinating to see this ancient idea of spheres of existence found in Buddhism starting to take hold in theoretical physics today.

CHAPTER 6

Life in a multidimensional universe

There is a guiding and directing
principle ad extrema, which interacts
with the material of the physical
universe but is not of it.

Sir Oliver Lodge

A few years ago I was interviewed on the radio on the subject of alien life, together with Britain's Astronomer Royal, Sir Martin Rees. I was delighted to discover that, far from the closed-minded attitude to this subject that I had come to expect from someone in his position, Sir Martin said we should consider the possibility of life on other planets in this solar system, including Mars, Venus, Jupiter, and Saturn. When Dr King pioneered such views in the 1950s, he was mercilessly ridiculed for them. But then, the greatest revelations of history have always disturbed the apparent certainties of contemporary thinking.

The theory of multidimensional existence would, at one time, have been scoffed at by the scientific community as being the domain of weird mysticism. Now it is a central plank of modern theoretical physics. Such concepts as string theory and parallel universes suggest that there are many levels of existence beyond the purely physical. This leads to the possibility of life on planets that are physically uninhabitable by us, and where the life may be undetectable to us. The serious acceptance of time travel, speeds faster than light, invisible matter, and dark energy has radically altered our whole approach to UFOs and the idea of life on other planets generally.

Some scientists are open-minded enough to think beyond that which may be termed physical reality. Professor Klaus Heinemann, a German-born theoretical physicist, is one such scientist. He has for many years worked in experimental physics under contract to NASA, and is a former research professor at Stanford University. He has written papers and lectured extensively on the commonly perceived rift between science and spirituality, and eventually founded the Eloret Corporation, which conducts scientific research in a range of fields, including computational fluid dynamics and nanotechnology.

In addition to being an established figure in more conventional areas of science, Heinemann is open to investigating otherworldly phenomena and, in particular, devotes considerable time to researching the significance of so-called orbs. These are plasma-like, translucent spheres of light, which are said to have been captured by digital cameras. This phenomenon came to his attention in 2004 when he and his wife, who were both attending a conference on energy medicine, were taking digital photographs and in some of them, these orbs appeared. In recent years, Heinemann has worked on finding out more about the images that digital cameras can detect but that are invisible to the human eye. He notes that we can see only a minuscule fraction of what we call reality with our physical eyes and the remainder of the huge electromagnetic spectrum is invisible to us.

The electromagnetic spectrum includes gamma rays, X-rays, ultraviolet radiation, the visible spectrum, infrared radiation, microwaves, and radio waves. The only difference between any of these is their wavelength or frequency. The radiation is continuous but for practical reasons scientists made divisions, and these were established mainly by the limitation of available techniques used to detect wavelengths. I recently had a conversation about visible and invisible matter with award-winning journalist and writer Hazel Courteney, a good friend, while she was working on her new book, *Countdown to Coherence*. In the course of her research she had interviewed several well-established scientists, including Professor Heinemann and material physicist Professor William A. Tiller, and she gave me an illustration that they use of the size of the visible light spectrum. If you imagine the electromagnetic spectrum as a reel of film 2,500 miles long, the portion that most people can see, unless you are highly sensitive, is approximately two frames, or two inches.

The light that our eyes can see is that part of the electromagnetic spectrum that consists of the colors of a rainbow. Each of these colors corresponds to a different wavelength of light. The other electromagnetic waves—radio waves, infrared light, ultraviolet light, X-rays, gamma rays, and microwaves—are invisible to our eyes. So much activity and radiation beyond our visible perception suggests that other forms of energy and matter exist, undetected by current science.

What does this mean in terms of the existence of unseen (i.e. not physically visible whether by the naked human eye or through high-powered telescopes) planets, and different levels or frequencies of life on other planets? Closer to home, could science be starting to detect—in the form of orbs and other phenomena—life on this Earth that cannot be physically seen, but is visible to a clairvoyant, and to provide a rationale for its existence? For years, the aura has been successfully photographed using Kirlian photography, a technique developed in 1939 by Russian inventor and researcher Semyon Kirlian together with his wife, Valentina. Now some theoretical physicists are starting to explore an area that has all too often been mentioned only as a somewhat vague, psychic explanation. I must say that my teacher, Dr King, was an exception in this respect. He clearly and explicitly stated repeatedly that other levels of existence were not just nebulous spheres of spirituality. He described them as being as physical as our material realm, but vibrating at a different frequency of energy.

Based on several years of experiments, Heinemann's current working theory is that orbs are emanations from spirit beings. He says that there has always been considerable anecdotal evidence that the spirit world exists, but now, with digital technology, he thinks we are seeing it. The implications for the way we view our world, and physical death, are enormous. So too, I suggest, are the implications for finding out about life on other planets.

The growing acceptance of such research was reflected at the world's first conference on the orbs phenomenon, which took place in May 2007 in Sedona, Arizona, and brought together prominent scientists and researchers in this subject. Experts stated their belief that the orbs demonstrate good evidence of otherworldly life forms.

Hazel Courteney, who has spent years researching this fascinating field, maintains that there is scientific evidence for phenomena that have been previously considered impossible. In an article she wrote for the British newspaper the *Daily Mail* in July 2007, she quotes Professor Heinemann as saying that the photographs of these orbs were as close to scientific proof as we have ever come to proving the existence of spiritual reality. Heinemann is part of a growing group of scientists involved in researching the nature of consciousness, and investigating what is known as the "invisible spectrum."

Professor Tiller spent more than forty years at Stanford researching the nature of consciousness. At the Tiller Foundation in Arizona, his current line of inquiry focuses on psychoenergetic science, demonstrating that human consciousness and sustained intention are together capable of significantly affecting both the properties of materials (nonliving and living) and what we consider to be physical reality. The results of his research in this field have indicated that there are two distinct levels of physical reality and not just one. This discovery alone could lead to us accepting more of the invisible than we do at present. Tiller states that the second level of physical reality functions in the empty space between the fundamental particles that make up our normal atoms and molecules. As such, it is currently invisible to us and to our traditional measurement instruments.

Once again this concurs with views expressed some fifty years ago by Dr King that the space between atoms is composed of etheric matter in which psychic (higher frequency) emanations are stored. Science is now starting to validate concepts that used to be written off as so much mumbo-jumbo, although plenty of scientists are still contemptuous of them. However, a growing number are breaking free from the sterile, blinkered thinking that besets their more orthodox colleagues. Heinemann and Tiller are among this number and are to be commended for their open-mindedness.

The work being carried out by Tiller involves serious experimental and theoretical study in the field of subtle energy and intention, the results of which he has published in several papers and lectures. Heinemann has been reported as giving full recognition to Tiller's work, which he feels offers good evidence of realities beyond those we can actually see. Tiller points to the virtually limitless number of frequencies and the realities that could potentially exist in them. Their worlds would appear as real to their inhabitants as ours does to us. Hazel Courteney believes that some people can travel between such realities, and has concluded that time is a space that we can navigate, as she elaborates in her book.

A good example of changing attitudes in science can also be found in the work of leading theoretical physicist, American-born Dr Michio Kaku. Often seen on television, he is currently a professor at City College of New York where he has lectured for more than twenty-five years. Dr Kaku has investigated, and written about, the idea that many universes—termed parallel universes and multiverses—exist independently of us. He examines subjects that, although not considered possible today, could be possible in the future, such as the technologies of invisibility, teleportation, precognition, star ships, antimatter engines, time travel, and more. In my view, such things not only are possible but have already been happening in our world, and especially in the worlds beyond.

In 2003, he gave a significant interview to a journalist in which his views were reported as follows. Physicists, he said, no longer believe in a universe, but instead in a multiverse, where many universes exist simultaneously. Interestingly, he pointed out that the multiverse idea allows us to combine into a coherent picture the Judeo-Christian idea of creation occurring at an instant of time and the Buddhist idea of timelessness. In his view, there was nothing in the beginning except hyperspace—perhaps ten or eleven dimensional, and unstable because of the quantum principle, which meant there were fluctuations in the nothing that existed. Bubbles began to form in this nothing, and these bubbles began to expand rapidly, giving us the universe. He sees this process of expansion of the universe as being similar to boiling water, when tiny bubbles form and begin to expand rapidly.

I would add that this is even closer in some ways to the ancient Hindu idea, found in yoga philosophy, of creation being an out-breathing of the divine from a state of potential into a state of manifestation. In Hindu thought, though, this expansive process depicted by an out-breathing is followed by an in-breathing in which everything returns back to its divine source. That is what gives meaning and purpose to life—to gain experience within manifestation and then to return all-knowing to divinity. Once again, we can see that science is inevitably entering the province of philosophical and religious thought. It shows that there can be no lasting division between science and religion.

In the same interview, Kaku theorized that different realms of existence actually coexist with our current physical realm, even though we cannot see, feel, or touch them. He described this as decoherence, with many worlds in which different experiences are taking place. He gave the example of sitting in a room, listening to a radio. While you listen, many frequencies exist simultaneously all around you in the room, although your radio is tuned to just one frequency. In the same way, in the same space, there could be the wave function of different life forms having multitudinous experiences in different places and possibly times. All of this coexists, but in your sitting room, you are tuning in to one radio channel, which is your reality channel, where you exist. He added that communication with these different universes could, in the future, be our salvation.

Kaku expressed some strident views on the SETI program (referred to in Chapter 3), making the point that an alien race who could reach our planet would, by definition, be vastly more technologically advanced than we are, and surmising that we might not even recognize their presence in our galaxy. He likened humanity to ants in an anthill. The ants would not understand, or be able to make sense of, a ten-lane superhighway next door, the equivalent of a civilization created by an advanced race of alien visitors. Bluntly, he says that we would not be smart enough to find it. Incidentally, this analogy goes a long way to answering the question: Why don't they come down here and land openly among us? It is interesting to note that Professor Kaku has come to the conclusion that we have a lot to learn about ourselves before we can begin to understand the reality of other dimensions and planetary races that exist around us. He could be tapping some very important principles about life on other planets, which may not be discovered and contacted so much through physical means as by what could be regarded as metaphysical ones, i.e. through an acceptance of multilevel existence as well as interplanetary life.

Another area of scientific study that impacts on interplanetary life is research into invisible matter. The mainstream scientific organization Fermilab, which is located near Chicago, Illinois, and is a US Department of Energy national laboratory specializing in high-energy particle physics, is conducting cutting-edge research on dark matter and dark energy. According to scientific sources, the present universe is composed of some 96 percent dark matter and dark energy, and only 4 percent atoms or visible matter. It is currently continuing to expand, and is, in their view, likely to expand forever, whatever "forever" means. These scientific sources have concluded that dark energy must exist—even though it has not been physically detected—from the fact that the expansion of the universe is accelerating. Dark energy is regarded as some kind of hidden force that must be pushing galaxies apart from each other to bring about this expansion. Dark matter is a theoretical concept that is now seen as vital to our understanding of the universe. It is thought to hold the galaxies together since without it there is not sufficient mass to generate the necessary gravitational forces.

It is easy to dismiss theoretical physics as unproven and therefore not worthy of consideration, but that would belie its value. Black holes, for example, were originally a theoretical concept allowed for in the theory of relativity, and are now regarded by scientists as proven fact. White holes, which are also allowed for in relativity, are the exact opposite of black holes, i.e. they spew out matter rather than drawing it in. Some people believe that white holes were the cause of creation itself and that the possible existence of numerous white holes could lead to the existence of numerous universes or multiverses. But their existence is yet to be proven.

Another very interesting concept, as yet unproven, is the cosmic wormhole. This was first known as the Einstein-Rosen Bridge, after a collaboration between Einstein and his long-time colleague Nathan Rosen. It arose from the idea of black holes, which are caused by a star collapsing to the point of zero volume and infinite density known as "singularity." The intense gravitational field so created absorbs all matter and even light in its vicinity, never to reappear again. The Einstein-Rosen Bridge joins two distant regions of space-time through a spatial shortcut, acting as a bridge between a black hole and a white hole. This idea has developed, mainly through science fiction, into a space tunnel through which, because of the gravitational forces at work, it would be theoretically possible to travel at speeds faster than light. Such a journey could not only be through space but also through time. In theory, you could travel hundreds of years into the past, or even the future, through a cosmic wormhole.

This in turn leads to philosophical dilemmas as well as physical and technological challenges. Scientists debate, for example, the so-called "grandfather complex." This explores the somewhat gruesome anomaly that if you could go back in time, you could theoretically kill your grandfather and thereby prevent your own birth. Some scientists have concluded that there would have to be some universal law to prevent this impossibility taking place and, in my view, they thereby concede that, at some point, the laws of physics must be governed by some overarching spiritual principle, which establishes what can and cannot happen in space and time. I would see this as the law of karma, because it is this that determines our cycle of experience.

These mind-boggling areas now being explored in physics and astrophysics require, in my view, the scientist to enter the terrain of the metaphysician. Those scientists who believe in the existence of invisible matter of one kind or another are, after all, confirming the long-held view of psychic researchers. Perhaps those pioneers of the late nineteenth and early twentieth centuries, who explored the psychic world and were pilloried by their more orthodox contemporaries for doing so, are now being vindicated by some of these discoveries. Mind you, even some of them would perhaps have been surprised that the percentage of invisible matter in the universe is believed to be as high as it is.

One of these pioneers was British scientist Sir Oliver Lodge, known for his work in connection with electromagnetic waves and radiotelegraphy, who claimed to have proved scientifically that life goes on after death. Lodge was one of the foremost English physicists, distinguished in electricity, a pioneer in wireless telephony, and a Fellow of the Royal Society, who nevertheless devoted much of his time to psychic research and the importance of a spiritual overview of the sciences. To him, it was not either one or the other, but both. He said, "Life and mind never were functions of the material body. They only displayed themselves by means of the material organism." This confident assertion, coupled with the work of other investigators into mediumship, did not change the thinking of most people. The joint efforts of the church and materialistic scientists suppressed and discredited the researchers' findings, aided and abetted by a significant number of well-publicized cases of fraud and deception by mediums, which were leapt upon by the skeptics. So, despite many convincing research projects, the mediumship-based theory of the survival of consciousness remained a minority belief.

In the later decades of the twentieth century, however, an increasing number of academic institutions set up departments, or sub-departments, to undertake research and run courses in paranormal phenomena. Institutes and trusts were formed, offering facilities for parapsychologists to meet and share their findings. One prominent researcher is Gary Schwartz, professor of psychology, medicine, neurology, and psychiatry at the University of Arizona. Like many others, he started out being very skeptical of mediumship, and carefully designed a series of projects to investigate the veracity of mediums' claims to have contacted people who had died. In a quest to explore what he called "the living soul phenomenon" Dr Schwartz conducted a series of tightly controlled and rigorous research studies of the interaction between sitters and mediums. The aim was to establish the accuracy of information produced by the mediums. In one study, the mediums achieved 83 percent accuracy, in another, 77 percent without any verbal input whatsoever from the sitters.

Schwartz used a triple blind procedure in one of his studies, i.e. none of the participants in the project—the mediums, the sitters, and the experimenters—had any means of knowing who was giving readings to whom. The sitters had substitutes, so that there was no possibility of mediums picking up nonverbal cues, psychically tuning in to the sitter, or using mind reading. The sitters were eight students who had recently been bereaved, and the eight mediums were chosen for their previously assessed accuracy. In each case, the medium was not told the sitter's or the deceased person's identity. According to Schwartz, the results showed that mediums can receive accurate information about deceased individuals.

If life on this Earth is not restricted to the physical body, there is no reason to suppose it would be anywhere else in the universe. From my own channeling experiences, and having given hundreds of psychic readings and trained others to do so, I know beyond any doubt that there are higher realms of existence around this world. However, many people will not believe such things until they are confirmed by scientists.

Dr Sam Parnia undertook a number of research projects at Southampton Hospital with patients who had suffered cardiac arrest, some of whom had had near-death experiences (NDEs). An NDE is when a person who has technically died continues to be conscious of what's going on around them. Patients in one study recalled watching events that had occurred in the middle of a cardiac arrest, which had been subsequently verified by medical and nursing staff. Parnia concludes that for this to have happened, consciousness must have been maintained even though, according to the monitoring instruments, the brain was, at best, severely disordered and, at worst, not functioning at all. Even more significant to the acceptance of multidimensional life, many reported out-of-body experiences (OBEs), which they were able to describe. Typically, these involved traveling through, or seeing, a tunnel of light and experiencing a feeling of great peace. In one case, a patient described seeing her deceased father standing in what appeared to be a door frame, and telling her to go back, which she did and was resuscitated.

Even though the NDE patients' brains were incapacitated, which in normal circumstances leads to loss of memory, they had very clear recall of their experiences. People who are so severely ill that they have reached the clinical point of death have somehow been able to report having lucid, well-structured thoughts and experiences. There are also reliable anecdotes of patients who have recalled detailed events that have taken place during resuscitation. According to Parnia, NDEs show clear thought processes when the brain is at best severely disrupted and, in all likelihood, not functioning. He and other scientists take this to indicate that consciousness is not limited to the physical brain, and may not even be derived from it. Some would go further and say that certain NDEs show that we exist after death and have a psychic or spiritual body as well as a physical one from which an OBE can take place.

There have been countless cases of OBEs, not just during NDEs. Floating above the physical body and looking down on it prior to going to sleep is a common one. Traveling to other locations, either in this physical realm or in another realm, has sometimes been reported, and encounters with deceased relatives or angelic beings can be real and tangible events in the lives of those who experience them. I have undergone an OBE on more than one occasion. One time, I was able to identify the detail of a wallpaper pattern in relation to a particular picture in a room in a neighboring building. The next day I confirmed it by going there and checking the accuracy of what I had seen. Although I was familiar with this room, I had never made that particular observation before. I have no doubt whatsoever that OBEs occur, and I give an example of a particularly significant one from a mystical point of view in the next chapter.

If it's possible to exist out of the body on this Earth, why not on other planets, too? Indeed, the whole realm of existence on another planet may be out of body, as far as we are concerned, because it is happening at another frequency and would be invisible and undetectable to us. Multidimensional life throughout the universe is increasingly being addressed by scientific researchers but to understand it in greater depth, it is mysticism we need to turn to now, rather than the mathematically driven world of theoretical physics and other scientific disciplines.

CHAPTER 7

Mysticism and the Masters

Mysticism has been in the past, and
probably ever will be, one of the great
powers of the world.

W.B. Yeats

D eep in the forests of the Yucatan Peninsula in Mexico can be found the remains of monuments and buildings constructed by the Mayans. Their civilization is said to have lasted almost three thousand years and their land extended to present-day southern Mexico, El Salvador, Guatemala, Belize, and western Honduras. It peaked in the tenth century CE and then started to decline until suddenly, for reasons about which historians still speculate, vanished some seven hundred years ago. Nobody could convincingly argue that the Mayans were civilized and peace-loving, certainly by the time of their demise. They engaged in ritual human sacrifice to their gods with bloodthirsty regularity and were steeped in a culture of cruelty, but they were exceptionally advanced in the field of astronomy. Their extraordinarily accurate calculations enabled them to create a calendar said to be more precise in certain respects than the calendar we use today. This calendar ends at the time of the winter solstice on December 21 2012.

Following the arrival of the Spanish conquistadors, most of their writings were destroyed as being "works of the devil." However, four codices were salvaged, of which the most important is the Dresden Codex. Written on flattened fig bark and covered in lime paste, this is just over three yards in length and since the eighteenth century has been kept at the Royal Saxon Library in Dresden. Its contents are apocalyptic. In its last chapter, it is said to indicate the end of the world through rains coming from black clouds in the sky as well as lightning. Is this an early prediction of global warming, or possibly a reference to the black rain connected with nuclear fallout? Although they cannot be linked definitively, many people believe that this is a warning tied in to the end of the Mayan calendar in 2012.

The Hopi Indians from North America, whose culture is estimated to have been in existence since 500 BCE, also believed in a devastating period ahead—a time of intense trial, marked by overwhelming social, environmental, meteorological, and political problems, leading up to the end of the world. Such cataclysm will be heralded by what they refer to as the appearance of a "blue star spirit." All is not lost, however, for they see a message of hope in a location they refer to as Prophecy Rock in Arizona, which indicates that humanity will have a choice to make. They say that death from these catastrophic events is not inevitable, if people change sufficiently.

Scholars pore over ancient religious documents, including the Jewish Torah, the New Testament Book of Revelation, and Vedic writings, all of which are said to contain warnings of the coming apocalypse. Egyptian hieroglyphics in the great pyramids are also said to give such warnings. Some see portents in the Jewish calendar, which indicate that the time for these occurrences is very close at hand. This tallies with the views of many environmental campaigners around the world, who would not necessarily describe themselves as being mystical.

Perhaps the greatest, and certainly the best known, western prophet is Nostradamus. His quatrains, which still fill the shelves of bookshops right across the globe, make for dire reading. Many see his references to intense heat in the sea, great drought, famine, boiling lakes, and fire from the sky, as prophesying global warming and nuclear fallout. Some see clear indications that the period he is referring to in these prophecies is the modern day, but there is some hope to be found there, too. Possibly one of his most famous prophecies, which established him for a while at the court of France, was his warning to Henry II that he could die in a jousting accident. Nostradamus went on to say that Henry could be a great figure of unity for his people, and the very fact that Nostradamus warned the king was, I believe, to try to prevent the jousting accident from happening. Much to the consternation of the queen, Henry did not follow this advice, and he died exactly as Nostradamus had predicted. As with a personal prophecy, so with global predictions: They are given to help us to change. If we continue unabated in the direction we are now going, the dire doomsday scenario seen by Nostradamus and others might come to pass. However, if we change, it could be averted.

On the whole, the great mystics of history have tended to work behind the scenes, following a subtle plan rather than openly revealing themselves and their full powers for all to see. Among these, a relative handful of men and women from all races and religious backgrounds have attained such a level of spiritual perfection that they no longer require the evolutionary lessons of this Earth. Having mastered all the basic lessons of the human experience cycle, they were ready to move on. Some of these have chosen to remain on this planet in order to save humanity—or help humanity to save itself—dwelling in secret retreats around the globe. They no longer need to die and be reborn, but remain in the same, ageless bodies, sometimes for many centuries. They are known as the Ascended Masters. This is reflected in the East in the tradition of enlightened souls, known as Bodhisattvas, which is connected with Buddhist thought in Tibet, China, Japan, Mongolia, and elsewhere. The most elevated Bodhisattvas are considered to be advanced individuals who could have escaped the cycle of rebirth and entered a divine state, but instead have chosen, out of their profound compassion, to remain on Earth in ageless bodies. They are, in other words, Ascended Masters. The fact that there are those among us who can live for extended periods in the same body without seeming to age has been recognized throughout the centuries, with different explanations in different cultures. In all of them, they have no need to remain on Earth because there is nothing for them to learn in this very ordinary and limited world.

Usually, they operate behind the scenes on behalf of humanity, but just occasionally, they live and work among us. Perhaps the best known Ascended Master to do so in recent times is Count Saint Germain. It is extremely difficult to get to the bottom of the many references to him that can be found in mystical, alchemical, and hermetical sources, but I have no doubt that he really existed and still does. One of the claims attributed to him, which I consider perfectly credible, is that he traveled astrally from his body while staying in the district of Naples and Mount Vesuvius in Italy. He allegedly describes this experience in *La Très Sainte Trinosophie*, which translates as *The Very Holy Trinosophia*, but is generally referred to as *The Most Holy Trinosophia*. A number of researchers and metaphysicians have alluded to this eighteenth-century manuscript, but a mist surrounds the various claims to have discovered the original.

In the library in Troyes, France, a document purporting to be *La Très Sainte Trinosophie* is said to have been copied from the original by Count Alessandro di Cagliostro (1743–95), who was allegedly a disciple of Count Saint Germain. Although the reputation of Cagliostro has been besmirched and he is often regarded as a fraudster and an imposter, others, including myself, do not hold this view. One champion of Cagliostro was none other than the great theosophist Madame Blavatsky, who also attracted far more than her fair share of detractors. In fact, it would be rare to find a prominent mystic in history who has not been attacked or defamed in some way. Cagliostro tried to disseminate his mystical knowledge and beliefs to all levels of society, reputedly gave healing to many thousands of people, and attempted to distribute knowledge of positive, Egyptian magical practice through freemasonry. His wish was to spread occult truths as widely as possible, and thereby improve the lot of humanity.

He did not mix just in high society, as would generally have been done not only by a Count, but also by successful alchemists and mystics of that period. He traveled Europe with his wife, Seraphina, demonstrating his powers and, according to some accounts, helping people from all walks of life, the sick and the poor included. For this, he was vilified and ultimately imprisoned by the Inquisition in Castel Sant'Angelo in Rome, and later in the fortress of San Leo in Tuscany, where he died a gruesome death. His work was not only diametrically opposed to the religious and political establishment of his day, it also went against the traditional practice of mystics through the ages, who tended to keep their knowledge secret. Perhaps he broke some ancient principle by sharing mystical truths with people of all stations, and several countries, who were not ready for it. If so, it was an admirable and, in my view, well-intentioned error. Perhaps he lacked the wisdom and psychological insights of the great Ascended and Cosmic Masters, who are aware of the impact such knowledge will have on humanity when it is proved in the right way.

The copy Cagliostro is said to have made of *La Très Sainte Trinosophie* was possibly done without the permission of Count Saint Germain, and may be another example of his eagerness to make important metaphysical knowledge available to everyone. If so, he succeeded in that aim. My wife, Alyson, and I have physically handled and read this document in the library in Troyes, although it is not generally accessible and special permission is needed to view it. The following short excerpt has been translated into English by my colleague and friend, Mark Bennett. (Mark has added punctuation where he considered it appropriate.)

Scarcely had I reached the surface of the Earth when my invisible guide led me even more quickly, the speed with which we covered distances through the air can be compared with nothing but itself; in an instant I had lost sight of the plains which I was so far above ... I had observed with astonishment that I had come out of the womb of the Earth far from the countryside around Naples. A deserted plain and some massive triangular shapes were the only things which I had caught sight of. Soon, despite the ordeals I had suffered, a new terror assailed me, the Earth seemed to me nothing more than a muddled cloud, I had been raised to an immense height. My invisible guide left me and I went back down. For quite a long time I rolled through space; already the Earth spread out before my troubled eyes ... I was able to calculate how many minutes would pass before I would be smashed against a rock. Soon, swift as thought, my guide speeds after me, he takes hold of me again, takes me away once more, he lets me fall back down, finally he takes me upward with him to an immeasurable distance, I was seeing globes turn around me, earths revolve at my feet ...

This extract describes a guided out-of-body experience in which Count Saint Germain traveled into space and witnessed the trajectory of other planetary bodies.

If it's possible to travel around this world in an out-of-body form, as discussed in the previous chapter, there is absolutely no reason why an advanced mystic could not travel far beyond it, deep into outer space. It would take an extraordinary individual to be capable of such a feat and I have no doubt that the Count was such a personage. He applied his ancient wisdom to the affairs of the world, planting seeds of progress in many fields of life. He was described by Voltaire in a letter to Frederick the Great as "a man who was never born, who will never die, and who knows everything." Some say this was a tongue-in-cheek comment, others that Voltaire had an unbounded admiration for the Count. Either way, intentional or not, I believe it to be a very perceptive remark.

While the concept of Ascended Masters has become accepted in much metaphysical teaching, Cosmic Masters are not yet so widely recognized. The key to understanding Cosmic Masters lies not just in marveling at their technological feats, although, as we have discovered in earlier chapters, these are stupendous, but also in appreciating their profound spirituality, wisdom, and mystical power. In the modern world, a strong distinction is made between scientist and mystic, but it was not always so. In former times, these two were united in one persona as the alchemist.

In fourteenth-century France, the legendary Nicholas Flamel, whose name has been brought to public attention recently in the Harry Potter books, pursued the ancient practice of alchemy, either alone in his laboratory or with his wife, Perenelle. So successful was he in turning base metal into gold that the Flamels became extremely wealthy citizens in Paris. Their previous income as booksellers had been satisfactory, but they were by no means prosperous. Then they became so rich that they were able to build several hospices for the poor and sick, purely at their own expense. This change in their financial worth has been attributed entirely to their success in the practice of alchemy. But despite their new-found wealth, the Flamels did not indulge themselves in the fourteenth-century equivalent of a sports car, a yacht, and a private jet. On the contrary, they maintained an extremely frugal lifestyle and continued to devote all their available time to the painstaking pursuit of what is known in alchemical circles as the Great Work.

To see the Flamels as a couple who "made it" because they became rich, or even as a couple of high esteem because of their undoubted charitable contributions to the needy, would be to miss the main point. Nicholas Flamel was a mystic through and through. He was not interested in gold for its physical properties, or even value. He understood that if he was to indulge himself with a materialistic lifestyle, as he could so easily have done, he would lose the powers he had gained. His goal was a spiritual one—all the rest was an extremely beneficial corollary of this, which he put to the best possible use as his ethical code demanded of him. While the story of Nicholas Flamel is sometimes dismissed as an exaggerated myth, this may not be the case. Having visited his former home in Paris where he had his laboratory, my impression is that the work of Nicholas Flamel was of great significance and that it would be foolish to dismiss it as nonsense. The practice he was engaged in was to him, and to many others, just as scientific as it was magical.

The same is true of Sir Isaac Newton. The hundreds of hours of diligent, intense work that he devoted to the practice of alchemy may, on the face of it, have seemed like a fruitless diversion from his main task. Surely, one might think, it was the laws of gravity, perpetual motion, and so forth that really mattered, not some arcane practice of turning lead into gold, which from all accounts ended in failure anyway. But alchemy is a science of consciousness as well as physicality. It is a powerful, transforming symbiosis of the experimenter and the object of his experimentation. Ironically, the advent of quantum physics reintroduced this idea that the mind of the experimenter could affect the outcome of the experiments, and thereby turned Newtonian certainties of physics on their head. Perhaps Newton instinctively knew this. Perhaps he realized that more was required of him than just to deal with physical observations and material deductions. Perhaps his great devotion to alchemy was not so much a distraction as an enabler. In short, perhaps it was his mysticism that drove him, inspired him, and helped to bring those flashes of realization that altered our view of the physical world forever.

Another towering English figure who turned his mind to science and mysticism was Sir Francis Bacon. Flying in the face of the Aristotelian approach, which, by then, had become universally accepted, Bacon advocated a very different methodology. Instead of using reason to deduce scientific fact, Bacon said that observation and experimentation should be the yardstick. He believed that man was the servant, an interpreter of nature, and that knowledge is the fruit of experience. In following this idea, he created the method that was to revolutionize the experimental process, known as scientific induction. There was far more to Bacon than this, however. He is thought to have been a great mystic and, secretly, a leading figure among the Rosicrucians. Undoubtedly, he was a wonderful essayist, lawyer, and philosopher, and some people, including me, believe that he contributed the most profound and florid passages to the plays and other works of his contemporary, Shakespeare. He was even a prominent politician, although his career as Lord Chancellor came to an abrupt, distasteful close, owing to what some believe to be trumped-up charges.

Perhaps it was Bacon's knowledge of mysticism that gave him the confidence and insight to refute centuries of accepted tradition, and surely he was right that intellectual reasoning alone is not sufficient to get to the truth. No one can deny the vast array of knowledge that the ancient Greeks bequeathed to the world. When they were right, they were impressively so, but it was sometimes a hit and miss process, although some of the misses may not have been as far off the mark as they seem. For example, one of the errors made by Aristotle was that he located the human brain in the heart rather than the head, but at a superphysical level, this is not as wrong as it appears. In yoga philosophy, all the chakras or psychic centers, which are located in the aura or etheric counterpart of humans, are regarded as being centers of mind, and one of the most significant of these is the heart chakra. The mystical element often associated with the heart center is air, which represents the mind.

Aristotle's philosophical lineage can, in fact, be traced back to mystical roots. He learned from Plato, who was a disciple of Socrates, who was said to be profoundly influenced by the teachings of Pythagoras. Although Pythagoras is known today for his theorem about the right-angled triangle, he combined in his teachings, which were expounded in the academy he founded in Croton in southern Italy, the synthesis of mathematics and mysticism. In those days, there were not the same distinctions as there are today between astronomy and astrology, numeracy and numerology, and so on. Pythagoras even brought music into the study of the heavens, and was one of the foremost experts on ritual, which he studied and practiced in his travels through much of the civilized world.

Just as Pythagoras had done, the alchemist combined science with mysticism, and was, in particular, a great proponent of the elements. These had nothing to do with the modern chemist's table but were a mystical key to understanding life. The alchemist was a believer not only in earth, fire, air, and water but, crucially, in a fifth element, known as ether. This element, within which all the others are contained, was the be all and end all for the alchemist. It was the key to the philosopher's stone—necessary to transmute metals into gold—and to the transformation of base matter into etheric substance. Is it the force that our cosmic visitors have understood, controlled, and harnessed to such a degree that they can enter the different frequency levels referred to in Chapter 6, and appear to blink in and out of existence in front of our very eyes? Is this the secret of dematerialization and rematerialization demonstrated before a crowd of witnesses in Voronezh in the Soviet Union by an alien being in 1989 as described in Chapter 3? Is this, even, what the "Star Wars" films were getting at with the famous catch phrase "May the Force be with you"?

Sir Oliver Lodge, for one, spoke and wrote eloquently about the importance of ether at the turn of the twentieth century. In the same period, another mysterious figure appeared on the scene in Paris. His name was Fulcanelli, although his true identity has been the subject of speculation and debate ever since. One thing that is widely believed about him, though, is that he was connected in some way with the Ascended Master Count Saint Germain. Two books by Fulcanelli emerged in twentieth-century Paris that were to become classic works in the alchemical genre. These were *Le Mystère des Cathédrales (The Mystery of the Cathedrals)* and *Les Demeures Philosophales (The Dwellings of the Philosophers)*. Including detailed and authoritative accounts of the meanings hidden within various depictions—that is carvings, drawings, sculptures, or paintings—to be found in or on significant buildings in Europe, they are said to be, for "he who has the eye to see," an initiation into the deeper, mystical philosophies of life. According to Fulcanelli, the symbols carved on Gothic churches and other structures reveal messages about the past, present, and even the future.

He saw indications that a great change will come to our world whether we like it or not. This would be an alchemical transformation of people, not just metal substances in a laboratory. Humanity would be given an opportunity, in what many would describe now as a New Age, to make the change or to resist it, but either way a transmutation would take place. The most obvious challenge that confronts us all is the transformation now underway in the environment and the inherent dangers that go with it. In tandem with this is the change of vibration at a mystical level, which is being enhanced and speeded up. One very significant and historic artifact identified by Fulcanelli is the Great Cross of Hendaye, situated in a small town in the Pyrénées-Atlantiques in southwest France. This stone cross, he believed, carried in the symbols engraved upon its sides a message about the great change to come, a dangerous period that would signal the end of the old and the start of the new. It would be the end of time as we know it. His ideas correspond to some of those described at the beginning of this chapter. In fact, warnings of impending disaster and the need for humanity to change are common themes among mystics.

Fulcanelli never appeared in public, even to his publisher, who received the manuscripts of these texts from his pupil, Eugene Canseliet. A meeting is supposed to have taken place between Fulcanelli and Jacques Bergier, a chemical engineer and journalist based in France, in 1937 in which Fulcanelli warned of the dangers of atomic experimentation and emphasized that, through alchemy, matter and energy could be manipulated to produce a field of force without the dangers inherent in nuclear power. This is a theme taken up with vigor, and in detail, in early claimed contacts with extraterrestrial beings, which may indicate that the science of the Cosmic Masters has far more in common with these cautious and secretive mystics than it does with some of their more materialistic counterparts. One piece of advice that Bergier claimed to have received from Fulcanelli about the philosopher's stone is that alchemy is not so much about the transmutation of metals as of the experimenter himself. Perhaps cosmic beings can be better understood through a study of the advanced mystics of this world, and the power they have obtained within themselves, which later manifests at an outer level.

Whoever Fulcanelli was in reality, he was undoubtedly an extraordinary individual, and he could well have been as versed in the physical sciences as he was in alchemy, hermeticism, and kabbalistic practice. He may have been a prominent Rosicrucian, who kept his other identity closely hidden, even from his closest associates, but could he also have been an agent for another, higher authority, namely, one of the most enigmatic personages in European history, Count Saint Germain? And could a being of the caliber of Count Saint Germain, who is widely accepted as being an Ascended Master, give us an indication of the true stature of those who come from other worlds? In fact, is an Ascended Master as close as it gets on this Earth to being a Cosmic Master?

Another extraordinary individual who may give some credence to this idea is Apollonius of Tyana. In the second century CE, the Roman Empress Julia Domna took as her personal secretary a writer by the name of Philostratus. One of the tasks she entrusted to him was the compilation of all available records that had been written about Apollonius by his student, Damis. One of the reports recounted by Damis illustrates not only supernormal but possibly technological powers. He describes a visit by Apollonius to the Himalayas where he met with sages who had extraordinary abilities. Their chosen dwelling place was covered by a strange fog, which appeared to give them some kind of protection. Apollonius concluded this because he learned that outside the perimeter of this fog men had fallen in their attempt to scale the perpendicular ascent, necessary to reach these elders, but inside it they had not done so. It sounds as though they had erected some kind of force screen, created from etheric matter, which protected those within it. In this respect it is reminiscent of science-fiction stories about UFOs and aliens, and indeed information gleaned through Dr King's cosmic contacts.

Apollonius, who was of Greek descent, was an outspoken teacher and he traveled extensively during the time when Christianity was first being disseminated. Like the early Christians, he was bitterly resented by some in the Roman establishment and eventually came to the attention of the Emperor Domitian. Arrested on a charge of treason, he was brought before the emperor and, in keeping with the custom at the time, given the opportunity to plead in his own defense. Instead of this, he berated Domitian for his misuse of power and then, just before the emperor could sentence him to death, disappeared. Some time later, he was said to be in Greece, teaching in public, when he suddenly stopped and declared that he was witnessing the end of the tyrant as though he was seeing it in front of his eyes. According to this report, that turned out to be the exact moment of Domitian's death. Such incidents have much in common with some of the capabilities attributed to the Cosmic Masters.

As well as walking this Earth and attempting to influence us to change our hearts and minds, not to mention our behavior—and ultimately our higher selves—in order to avert the coming catastrophe, Ascended and Cosmic Masters reach out to humans by channeling messages through mediums. In the West, in the late nineteenth century, Madame Blavatsky pioneered the process of revelation about these great beings in a very direct and far-reaching manner. She referred to some of them as Mahatmas, and spoke of El Morya, the Master Koot Humi, and perhaps most significantly of all, the Lord Maitreya. Her work was embraced and followed up by another pioneering lady of indomitable spirit, Alice Bailey. She too had communion with intelligences connected to what is known as the Spiritual Hierarchy of Earth. This Holy Order has also become known as the Great White Brotherhood, although this name does not refer to the race or sex of its members, who are not necessarily male or white. Dr King is among those to have claimed contact with Ascended Masters, and with careful discrimination, one can gain some understanding of this amazing body of elevated beings, who watch over, guide, and help us as and when they can, in our faltering steps toward a more enlightened world.

However, you need to be very discriminating when dealing with claims of contact with Ascended Masters. Just as UFO organizations have been infected with false and deluded claimants

—especially in relation to the abduction experience—so, too, has the field of channeling. At the same time as Fulcanelli was making his mark in Europe, an American by the name of Guy Ballard claimed to have had a very unusual experience on the other side of the world. While climbing Mount Shasta in California, he said that he had a direct contact with Count Saint Germain, whom he described as an ageless and wise Ascended Master. He also claimed that flying vehicles were kept underneath the mountain in a retreat where other Masters resided. The I AM movement, which he founded after his alleged contact, later fell into considerable disrepute. As with the UFO movement, though, fakery and delusion do not disprove the genuine claims, even if the claimant himself should later go "off the rails." Like moths around a flame, they only serve to illustrate the potency of the source they obscure.

The interference of dark forces is a more serious hazard than even hoaxing or self-deception. The association of the dark side with all things mystical, which was so carefully fostered by the church, is little different from the attempts by various government bodies to make all aliens seem hostile. The careful turning of the word occult from its original meaning of "hidden" into something evil is a clear demonstration of this. Some mystics played up to this plan, and in the twentieth century you could find, in the same organizations, extremely undesirable practitioners of negative magic rubbing shoulders with exponents of positive forces for good. Dion Fortune, for example, attempted to rally some of her colleagues and fellow magicians to use spiritual practices during World War Two to combat the wicked threat of Nazism, while other magicians were known to have direct connections with the Nazi party. Dion Fortune died shortly after the war from leukemia, and some attribute her untimely death at the age of fifty-six to what they see as her well-intended foolhardiness in openly coming into conflict with such forces.

There was, and still is, a code of secrecy among many in the mystical community, which is why much of their teaching was literally occult. In this respect, Count Saint Germain was radical. For a period in European history—especially the eighteenth and early nineteenth centuries—he lived, worked, traveled, and openly demonstrated some of the powers he had attained, using them in the interests of peace, humanitarianism, and the advancement of culture. As a refined, knowledgeable, and spiritual giant of a man, who lived for hundreds of years in the same physical body, he is well worthy of further study, if only to show what supernormal abilities can be gained by someone from this Earth, never mind a space traveler from beyond it.

In common with our extraterrestrial visitors, Ascended Masters will not at any time cross the line laid down by the law of karma. This means that they are incredibly restricted. In fact, it is a tragic paradox that the most enlightened intelligences who walk the Earth are also the most limited— not by themselves but by us. They understand one thing far more deeply than we do, and that is the inestimable value of experience. For all the pain it can cause us, they are not willing to rob us of this priceless gift and, even if they wish to at times, they are not permitted to do so.

Having delivered hundreds of lectures around the world relating to UFOs and extraterrestrial beings, the one question I can virtually guarantee will be asked is: "If they exist, why don't they land openly among us and prove themselves beyond all doubt?" I hope you have read enough in this book by now to accept that they could do so if they chose to, but like the Ascended Masters, our cosmic visitors are governed by divine and ineffable laws. They, too, regard experience as the greatest gift that even God can provide and will not take it away from us by forcing us to change. They will pick their moment for such a revelation, and it will be exact to the very second.

Such concepts as this are more for the mystical thinker than the intellectual speculator. All too often I have heard journalists, scientific pundits, and ufologists come up with a line of thinking that goes something like this: "Extraterrestrial beings cannot really be visiting our world because if they were, they wouldn't just give us little signs, such as a crop circle here, a sighting there, and the odd unsubstantiated contact. They would come straight to the point, arrive openly, and engage in communication at the highest governmental level, in an open and indisputable manner. Since they don't do this, they obviously don't exist." For this line of argument I would give one out of ten for psychology. It is patently ridiculous for a terrestrial person, who has no knowledge of genuine UFO contacts, to formulate a pattern of behavior that an extraterrestrial race is expected to follow and if they don't follow it, to assume that they don't exist. Following Baconian principles, we should look at what the evidence shows they actually do, rather than speculate about what we think they would or should do.

Although I would give it one of out ten for psychology, I would give it even less for mystical perception. The mystic knows that there is a lot more to realization than what goes on in the brain. Great beings, such as the Cosmic or Ascended Masters, know us far better than we know ourselves. They know that even if they convinced us through reason and demonstrated argument, this would not necessarily change our hearts, never mind our souls. To the mystic, the connection with the soul is of paramount importance. In yoga philosophy, this is often referred to as contacting our higher selves. Human psychology has developed a complex system for determining different behavioral patterns. All of these, for the yogi, boil down to two simple alternatives— those directed by the higher self, and those directed by the lower self. For example, a man who appears to be driven by ego could be motivated either by hunger for self-aggrandizement and personal power, or the desire to bring positive change to the lives of others. It may be a combination of both, but the predominant motivating impulse will come from either the higher or the lower self.

The Masters understand this far more than the most academically qualified psychologist does because they have mastered all the basic mental impulses within themselves. They are also in a position to know and understand the limitations of those who have not done so. How often have we known what we really should do in a given situation, but when it came to it, not done it? In western theology, this might be described as a sin, but as Paramahansa Yogananda used to say, a saint is a sinner who never gave up.

From a mystical point of view, consciousness is not just about our thoughts, or even our feelings. It is the energy within us at every level, which determines our responses to any given situation. Our lack of evolution in this respect has caused the Ascended Masters to have to wait patiently for thousands of years for a change to come. It has also held the Cosmic Masters back from more openly revealing themselves until humanity as a whole is psychologically prepared. This waiting game cannot last indefinitely because there are more important factors in the cosmos than whether we are ready or not, including the position of Mother Earth as a living intelligence, and these are now starting to impact upon us and bring our extraterrestrial visitors ever closer to our world. To the mystic, enlightenment is not a state of mental ability but a state of whole being. It is not just a change of ideas the Cosmic Masters are looking for, but a complete change of approach, which will enable them to come closer to this Earth. Change is required— and that change is upon us whether we like it or not.

"Fortune favors the prepared mind," said Louis Pasteur, and now is the time for preparations to be made with a greater urgency than ever before. You don't have to be mystical, or even psychic, to see the cataclysmic dangers that await earthly civilization unless some radical changes are made. There are widely differing viewpoints about the true nature and cause of the ecological disaster we face, and how soon it is likely to come, but no one can doubt that the world has never been a more dangerous place—certainly since the days of Atlantis and Lemuria, early civilizations referred to in many mystic writings. For one thing, we have nuclear power and with it the prolif-eration of nuclear weaponry. Once invented, these foul destructive weapons cannot be uninvented. Their devastating effects, should they be used, would be felt not only by everyone on the planet but by the planet itself and, potentially, have cosmic ramifications, too. No wonder this has been a recurrent theme from the 1950s onward among those who claim contact with aliens, and that the Cosmic Masters warned, through Dr King, of the terrible dangers wrought by splitting the atom. The only thing that can prevent nuclear weapons from being unleashed is a change of will among the people on Earth.

Even if our materialistically based civilization is not capable of communicating with, or ready to learn from, these otherworldly teachers, I believe that the more advanced members of the Spiritual Hierarchy of Earth have been eager to do so. In short, there has been on this Earth, for thousands of years, a collaborative plan between the highest and most advanced mystics here and the extra-terrestrials who watch over our progress with compassion and almost unbelievable patience.

This also explains why dark forces have gone to such lengths to distort the true message of the Cosmic Masters. Just as the presence of interplanetary beings would be wholeheartedly welcomed by the higher spiritual community on Earth, so it would be opposed by the lower, malev-olent entities who seek confusion, destruction, and conflict. Such entities would have no difficulty in deceiving people in their sleep state, or even under certain conditions while they were awake, into thinking that they had been abducted by hostile aliens who wished to perform unpleasant surgery upon them. They could certainly cause such people to believe that they had visited a space-craft and endured harrowing experiences, and the planted memory could emerge during a state of hypnotic regression, as discussed in Chapter 3. This could be a more complete explanation not only of how some so-called abductions took place, but also for certain Men in Black experiences, such as that of Albert Bender, who was lying down in his bedroom and feeling dizzy when he saw three shadowy MIB in his room. The witnesses could be perfectly genuine and fully believe that what they had experienced was contact with aliens from other worlds or MIB when it was really malevolent entities from lower realms of this world, deliberately trying to cause havoc within the UFO movement. These dark forces recognize the great spirituality of the Cosmic Masters, and wish to pervert it. The last thing they want is a New Age of peace and enlightenment on this Earth.

Not all psychic experiences that are allegedly connected to UFOs and extraterrestrials are unpleasant, though. One of the most celebrated current claimants is Miyuki Hatoyama, wife of

Yukio Hatoyama, who became Prime Minister of Japan in September 2009. She says that in the 1970s, while her body was sleeping, her spirit flew on a triangular-shaped UFO to Venus, which she described as extremely beautiful and very green. Whatever the truth of this—and I must repeat the importance of keeping an open mind—it certainly sounds like an astral experience of one kind or another and, from all accounts, an inspiring one.

To understand life on other planets, the mystic would say that you need to understand the concept of life on other planes. Then you are liberated from the idea that, because you and I could not live on Venus or Jupiter, nobody else could, or that because you and I cannot see life on Mars or the Moon, no life is there. William Blake, in the midst of the so-called age of enlightenment in the eighteenth century, openly claimed to practice what we would now call channeling, and attributed some of his elevated literary work to this. In fact, he said that a far greater abundance of his writings existed in the heavenly spheres than was available in this realm. It takes clairvoyance—psychic vision—to see those who have died and left their earthly physical bodies, but who are still very much alive. How much greater would your perception have to be to see the higher planes inhabited by more evolved races on other planets? That is assuming the beings who inhabit them wish you to see them and haven't used some kind of screening mechanism to prevent it.

To understand the Cosmic Masters it is, I believe, necessary to be conversant with the principles of mysticism, which have been with us throughout our history. If you wish to gain a real understanding about our extraterrestrial visitors, I suggest you look, not so much to the "nuts and bolts" fraternity, or those who have had a one-off encounter and been given a limited amount of information during it, but to a mystical source with an impressive track record who claims to have had genuine extraterrestrial contacts. One such mystic was the Swedish scientist, philosopher, and theologian Emanuel Swedenborg (1688–1772). He was a fascinating man who was highly regarded for his scientific inventions and other contributions to civilization. A late Renaissance figure, his talents included cosmology, natural science, engineering, mathematics, chemistry, and metallurgy, and he was extremely interested in all things philosophical, becoming well known in this field. He sat in the House of Nobility, and was active in the Riksdag (Swedish parliament) and the Swedish Royal Academy of Sciences.

In his mid-fifties Swedenborg had a deep spiritual awakening, which enabled him to perform the two practices that we know as channeling and astral projection. Among his later works was an extraordinary book for the time, *Earths in the Universe*. In this, he claimed to have received communications from what he called spirits on other planets, including Mercury, Jupiter, Mars, Saturn, and Venus. The book opens with an interesting description of the kind of communications he believed he was receiving in this latter period of his life.

1 **Inasmuch as, by the Divine mercy of the Lord,** the interiors which are of my spirit have been opened in me, and it has thereby been given me to speak with spirits and angels, not only with those who are near our Earth, but also with those who are near other earths; and since I had an ardent desire to know whether there were other earths, and to know their character and the character of their inhabitants; it has been granted me by the Lord to speak and have intercourse with spirits and angels who are from other earths, with some for a day, with some for a week, with some for months; and to be instructed by them respecting the earths from and near which they were, and concerning the life, customs, and worship of their inhabitants, besides various other things there that are worthy of note. And since it has been given me to become acquainted with these matters in this way, it is permitted me to describe them from the things which I have heard and seen. It is necessary that it be known that all spirits and angels are from the human race, and that they are near their own earths, and are acquainted with what is upon them; and that a man may be instructed by them, if his interiors are so far opened as to enable him to speak and be in company with them: for man in his essence is a spirit, and is in company with spirits as to his interiors; wherefore he whose interiors are opened by the Lord, is able to speak with them, as man with man. It has now been granted me to enjoy this privilege daily for twelve years.

2 That there are many earths, and men upon them, and spirits and angels from them, is very well known in the other life; for in that life, every one who from a love of the truth and consequent use desires it, is allowed to speak with the spirits of other earths, so as to be convinced that there is a plurality of worlds, and informed that the human race is not from one earth only, but from

numberless earths; and so as to be informed, besides, of what genius and life they are, and of what character their Divine worship is.

This is an amazing piece of writing by a highly respected eighteenth-century dignitary of immense scholarship. One key revelation he makes is that spirits and angels are from the human race, which I regard as his way of saying that they adopt humanoid form. This tallies with many of the descriptions of extraterrestrial contactees in modern times. It is also significant, and in keeping with mystical tradition, that Swedenborg defines the ability of an individual to communicate with such higher beings as being dependent on how far open are what he calls "our interiors." He gives more insight into this in the section of the book where he writes of his communications with spirits from Mars. These he describes as being "for the most part celestial men, not unlike those who were of the Most Ancient Church on this Earth." Is this another indication of a parallel between the Ascended Masters and the Cosmic Masters? His description of the channeling process with beings from Mars has the hallmark of authenticity and a genuine attempt to explain exactly how it feels to be on the receiving end, as the following passage shows:

Spirits from thence came to me, and applied themselves to my left temple, where they breathed their speech upon me, but I did not understand it. As to its flow it was very soft: I had never before perceived any softer; it was like a very gentle breeze. It breathed first upon the left temple, and upon the upper part of the left ear; the breathing proceeded thence to the left eye, and by degrees to the right, and flowed down afterward, especially from the left eye, to the lips; and when at the lips it entered through the mouth, and through a way within the mouth, and, indeed, through the Eustachian tube, into the brain. When the breathing arrived there, I understood their speech, and was enabled to speak with them. When they spoke with me, I observed that my lips were moved, and my tongue also slightly, which was owing to the correspondence of interior with exterior speech. Exterior speech is that of articulate sound which impinges upon the external membrane of the ear, and it is conveyed from thence, by means of the small organs, membranes, and fibers, which are within the ear, to the brain.

As someone who has considerable experience of practicing channeling for more than twenty-five years, albeit at an infinitely more lowly level than direct communication with Ascended Masters or interplanetary beings, this passage really has the ring of truth about it for me. One of the principles taught by Dr King is that the caliber of communicator that a medium can channel is relative to the spiritual attainment of that medium. This might be what Swedenborg is referring to when he talks about the interiors, or the degree to which the interiors are open. You could be an extremely effective medium, but be incapable of receiving communications from a highly evolved person in another realm of this Earth, never mind another planet. A medium might be brilliant at relaying messages from your deceased aunt with some accuracy, but simply unable to receive a message from one of the great saints or elevated geniuses of history, who are now in the higher realms. On the other hand, you could be a spiritually advanced individual who has not chosen to develop a channeling ability to a sufficient degree, in which case you could not be a medium for evolved beings with any great accuracy.

Swedenborg's essential claim to have been contacted by what he called spirits—in other words, higher frequency intelligences—from this solar system is a radical and extremely important one. I can certainly believe it. He was a most remarkable individual of outstanding mental capacity, but this does not necessarily mean that the communications he channeled were, word for word, received with a high level of accuracy. He did demonstrate, though, the important fact that mystical attainment can lead to direct telepathic communication with higher beings from other worlds. Hundreds of years later, one medium who did receive transmissions from the Cosmic Masters with an exceptionally high level of accuracy was Dr George King.

CHAPTER 8

Primary Terrestrial Mental Channel

Prepare yourself! You are to become the
voice of Interplanetary Parliament.

The Master Aetherius

E arly on the morning of April 25 1986, I awoke in the beautiful surroundings of a hotel that commanded panoramic views of Lake Powell in Arizona. I was part of a team led by Dr King and our task was to perform the Saturn Mission in cooperation with extraterrestrial beings. I was called to Dr King's room after breakfast and was with him when he received a message from an interplanetary communicator at 9.30 a.m. local time.

During this mental transmission, Dr King received instructions from a spacecraft designated Satellite Number 3 to activate some apparatus at The Aetherius Society's American headquarters in Los Angeles, in order to send out spiritual power to the world. This was to be the longest and most concentrated series of emergency operations of this apparatus—a spiritual energy radiator—that had been conducted up to that time, and it was to begin in thirty minutes' time (9 a.m. Los Angeles time). Exactly four hours and twenty-three minutes later, at 1.23 p.m. LA time, which was 1.23 a.m. on April 26 Moscow time, a tremendous explosion blew the roof and upper walls off a building housing a nuclear reactor. This was the catastrophe now generally referred to by the name of its location, the Chernobyl disaster, described as the worst nuclear reactor accident in history, and it occurred four hours and fifty-three minutes after an interplanetary communicator had warned Dr King of a pending emergency situation.

Unlike the Soviet atomic accident described in Chapter 2, the communicating intelligence did not reveal specific details about the location and severity of this emergency. In the 1958 incident, the description was given after the event, not before it. In 1986, something far more important than giving information was done—namely, a program of action was initiated to reduce the impact of this coming event. The operations using the spiritual energy radiator continued for several days, the last one taking place on April 29. This equipment had the capacity to receive and transmit energy sent through it by Satellite Number 3 for the benefit of humanity.

I know this sounds strange and will, for some, be difficult to believe, but I hope to have established by now that the incredibility of an event does not of itself make it untrue. The facts that subsequently unraveled speak for themselves. The Chernobyl disaster could and, according to many, should have been a far worse calamity than it was. In July 1986, The Aetherius Society published in its journal *Cosmic Voice* the fact that these emergency operations were performed to reduce the impact of the accident:

Shocking events which had been foreseen by the Cosmic Masters, who called upon their Primary Terrestrial Mental Channel—who had, in turn, activated his own resources of the Spiritual Energy Radiator and terrestrial equipment of the Saturn Mission in an outpouring of high-frequency, environment-stabilizing and life-saving Spiritual Energy, such as the world has seldom seen!!

In addition to publishing this news in the Society's journal within months of the accident occurring, we were not quiet in the media or on the public platform, that year or subsequently, about the extraordinary timing of this emergency operation. It was not until April 28 that the Soviet Union admitted the disaster had even occurred, and then only because radioactivity from it had been detected over Sweden. By then, The Aetherius Society under the leadership of Dr King had already been operational in direct cooperation with the Cosmic Masters for days.

Sixteen years later, on September 16 2002, the Russian journal *Pravda* published a most extraordinary report. This stated that while the explosion at Chernobyl on April 26 1986 was very large, it was luckily only a thermal blast. The fourth power-generating unit was basically destroyed by overheated steam but there was no nuclear explosion. At the time, the reactor contained approximately 180 tonnes of enriched uranium, and had a large blast occurred, half of Europe would currently not be depicted on any maps, it said. Even more remarkably, *Pravda* theorized that this apparent stroke of luck was due to help from a UFO, which had been seen by hundreds of people for some six hours, hovering above the fourth generating unit of the Chernobyl plant. An eyewitness described it as a ball of fire slowly flying in the sky, some twenty to twenty-six feet in diameter. He described how two rays of crimson light stretched toward the fourth unit while the object was some three hundred yards from the reactor. This event lasted for about three minutes before the lights from the UFO disappeared and it flew off in a northwesterly direction. *Pravda* concluded that the UFO brought the radiation level down, decreasing it by almost four times, and it was this that prevented a nuclear blast. The Russian journal surmised that alien beings are worried about the planet's environment, and in this, they could not be more correct.

This is a typical example of how the Cosmic Masters work. By communicating through a proven channel, Dr King, and receiving the cooperation of people in this world who act in the light of their warning, karma is manipulated for the benefit of humanity as a whole. This in turn enables such intelligences to intervene more directly in our affairs and, as in this case, save numerous lives and the environment as a whole from far worse destruction than actually occurred. Many tragic casualties resulted from the Chernobyl disaster, but even some of the most conservative commentators, who would not begin to accept a theory of extraterrestrial intervention, have concurred that it was amazing that the consequences for the world as a whole were, relatively, so small.

So how did Dr King find himself in the most unusual position of being a channel for our extra-terrestrial visitors? His story began on January 23 1919 in Lilleshall, a small village in the English county of Shropshire, where he was born in his grandmother's house. At the time, his grand-mother commented to his mother, Mary, that the child was not of this world. Those prophetic words, spoken by an exceptionally psychic lady, who was a medium in her own right, had a far greater significance than she could possibly have realized. George's father was a schoolteacher, who supplemented the family finances by working as an accountant for farmers and others in the local community. His mother, also clairvoyant, was a capable lady who specialized, among other things, in renovating and decorating houses and then selling them on. The King family, comprising George, his parents, and his younger sister, Mollie, lived in these houses while the work was going on, and so one of Dr King's most vivid memories of his childhood was the constant need to move, very often to a different part of rural England. This aspect of his childhood did not always give him fond memories, although he had a detailed recall of the communities in which he had lived. Having traveled with him, in a working and friendly capacity, to various parts of the UK, it was clear to me just how familiar he was with the English way of life, from the West Country to the North of England, and indeed with London, where he lived in his twenties and thirties.

One thing that marked out his youth was his avid interest in all things spiritual. In this he was fortunate to have the guidance of his mother and especially his grandmother. This lady is said to have acted as a medium for, among others, Lloyd George, who pioneered the welfare state as Chancellor of the Exchequer and later became Prime Minister. Dr King had a remarkable experience when aged eleven. His mother had been ill for some time, and one particular evening her condition appeared to have worsened. After the doctor had left, having done all he could for her, the young boy suddenly felt the urge to go out into the woods, even though it was dark, and a wild and windy night. On reaching the woods, he threw up his arms and put all his feeling into a prayer. While he was praying, the wind seemed to stop suddenly and all was silent.

He saw a white radiance, and in what appeared to be an iridescent ovoid, he could see a great and illuminated being, who told him to return home as his mother was now well. After this great being had departed, as quickly as it had arrived, the young boy ran straight home to find that his mother had recovered.

Brought up in the Anglican faith, it was not long before he felt the need to search more widely for the inner meaning of life. He became a devout Quaker for a while, and this was one of the factors in his decision, at the outbreak of World War Two, when he was aged twenty, to become a conscientious objector. The war was a formative influence on his life, as it was on all those who lived through it, especially those in the springtime of their years. George did not regard his stance as a ticket to his own safety or a way of keeping out of harm's way. On the contrary, he joined the fire service, becoming a section leader in London during the Blitz. The city was hit hard and he served with fearless dedication, a characteristic that he continued to display throughout his life. Although he was not willing to serve in the killing fields, he was very much engaged in the search and rescue fields, often entering blazing buildings to bring those inside to safety.

The effect of the war was to strengthen his quest for spiritual meaning. He had seen many pointless deaths, and helped save others through a combination of skill, leadership, and, in certain cases, clairvoyance—using that psychic vision, he was able to pinpoint where bodies might be found beneath the rubble and point his fire team in the right direction. Psychic powers were not enough for him, though. He wanted to know the real purpose of life and manifest the full potential of the spirit within. So, in the heady days of celebration coupled with austerity that marked out the postwar period in London, George King turned to the little-known field of yoga philosophy and practice.

Today, yoga is an accepted practice followed by millions of people who wish to improve their bodies, occasionally their minds, and, very exceptionally, their souls. Sadly, for some people it has become just another form of physical exercise rather than the complete science of self-realization, which it was originally conceived to be. The word yoga means, literally, union with God or the divine self within. Dr King practiced the physical asanas associated with hatha yoga rigorously and unsparingly but, in common with the yogis of old, who had performed these postures in retreats, caves, and secluded forests, he did so merely to prepare his body for the more advanced and far more profound practices of bhakti (devotion), raja (mental and psychic control), and gnani (wisdom). Of these, raja and gnani particularly attracted him in those days. Over a ten-year period, for eight hours each day he practiced the most advanced exercises available to a student in the West, including kundalini yoga, which for the uninitiated can be a dangerous thing to do. He dovetailed the whole of his life into his practice with a single-minded determination that I have found, from my studies of metaphysics and mysticism, to be unparalleled in the West. Devotees in the East practiced as rigorously as this, but they would break away from society to do so. To find an individual, who also had to work for a living, practicing alone in a turbulent place such as Waterloo station in London, with this kind of self-discipline, is exceptional.

At the time, practicing yoga was a far from accepted, or acceptable, way for a young man in conservative England to spend his time, but an individual with the open mind and inner drive of George King was not going to be put off by that. I well remember talking to his sister, Mollie, whom I know well, about this period in his life. She was also in London, working with great success in the theater. Apparently, the transformation in her brother took place overnight. She told me how he knew that one day he would need to go to America and he set his sights on perfecting the practice of yoga before then, and that he did so with a determination that was impressive even to kith and kin, who are not always renowned for recognizing such things about their loved ones. He had been able to obtain instruction through lectures, classes, and the literature that was starting to circulate more readily in the West, and year in, year out, he devoted himself to the more advanced practices.

To finance himself, he worked mainly as a taxi driver, although he took other jobs as and when necessary. He would tell his passengers, if they inquired, that he was driving to pay his way through university. When asked which university he attended, his reply would be "the university of life." Some people have questioned how a former taxi driver could be picked for the task of being Primary Terrestrial Mental Channel. The question is itself an inherently snobbish one, both socially and intellectually. You might just as well ask how a former carpenter, the Master Jesus, could be the son of God, or how a cowherd, Sri Krishna, could be the godlike being who produced some of the greatest teachings ever given to our world. In fact, Sri Krishna was also a driver, albeit of a chariot, when he delivered his epoch-changing philosophy to Arjuna, recorded in *The Bhagavad Gita*, which has reverberated through centuries of spiritual conduct.

Among the practices performed by Dr King during this period was the wonderful, ancient discipline of chanting Sanskrit mantra. He became adept, performing this practice for hours at a time, day after day, month after month, and year after year. He did this aloud, silently, and in his deepest inner being, bringing about vast changes within himself and in the environment around him. Another of the great practices at the very core of his disciplines was pranayama, or yoga breathing, which likewise he would do for extended periods of time, using ancient mudras (Tibetan hand signs) to enhance his level of attainment. He started to raise the mystic force referred to as kundalini, also known as the serpent power, and thereby awaken his chakras or psychic centers, bringing on great powers.

One of the fascinating stories he used to tell was of a levitation experience he had while living in a small apartment in Maida Vale, London. In those days, in common with many other young men, he would use Brylcreem on his hair. On one occasion, during one of his advanced practices, he found himself physically rising from the floor to the ceiling, brushing his head and leaving a greasy mark. His landlady noticed the mark and asked him one morning what it was and how it had arrived on the rather high ceiling of his room. He told her the simple truth, and then went off, as usual, to work. On returning home that evening, he found her sitting on the stairs, waiting for him, filled with curiosity to know just how the levitation experience had occurred. Some people may dismiss this story as fantasy, but levitation has been practiced for years, especially in eastern parts of the world.

It would not concern Dr King whether or not he was believed about this particular anecdote. His quest for inner realization and wisdom was more important to him than any powers he may possess, although he was actively engaged in using his healing skills to help others. He also practiced mediumship, working in conjunction with spiritualist groups, despite having reservations about some aspects of their tenets. For example, he was not a believer in mediumship being used to maintain family relationships with the deceased over a prolonged period. To him, it was a means of channeling teaching, healing, and protection for the benefit of others from those on "the other side." Among his guides, or communicating entities, was a Native American by the name of Gray Fox, who had such a physique that Dr King's own physical strength was demonstrably enhanced while he was overshadowed by him. Another was medical physician Sir James Young Simpson, and yet another, the scientist referred to in Chapter 6, Sir Oliver Lodge. Perhaps the most prominent of his guides during this period was a Tibetan master by the name of Chang Fu, who had suffered a very unusual death. He had been in a deep meditative state for about two years when a tribe of Mongols came along and found his body. Thinking he was dead and recognizing him as a master, out of great respect they made a funeral pyre and cremated the body, thereby preventing him from returning to this physical plane. He regarded it as a big mistake on his part, not foreseeing the possibility of his body being found. It does show the extraordinary detachment of an advanced eastern mystic, who chose to leave his body to inhabit a higher realm than this one for a prolonged period in his pursuit of enlightenment.

All this was a precursor to the mission that George King was destined to perform as Primary Terrestrial Mental Channel. The intense yoga practice was essential to reaching the level required to become a direct channel for the Cosmic Masters. Through that rigorous practice, he was able to achieve the intense focus necessary to eliminate virtually all error in his mediumship. In addition to this, it was vital for him to have an extremely high level of spiritual attainment, which was also brought about by this period of self-imposed training. These two abilities are combined —in fact, one tends to lead to the other—in the most profound state of meditation that can be entered by anyone, samadhi, and Dr King learned to induce it at will.

What a poor barometer of significance are the judgments made by contemporary society. We tend to forget, for example, that Christianity in its early days was not the famous and widely followed belief system that it was to become. When Jesus rode into Jerusalem for what turned out to be his crucifixion, Judas was required to identify him by that fateful kiss, specifically because he was not well known enough to be recognized. His followers were few in number, and for hundreds of years Christianity was regarded as just one of several cults, until it was picked up by Constantine the Great and turned into an official religion. A hundred and fifty years ago, if you were to have asked the people of Britain who would go down in history out of Palmerston, Canning, and Wilberforce, the likelihood is that Wilberforce, the only one not to have been prime minister, would have been last on the list. Today, he is probably the best remembered internationally because of his work on the abolition of the slave trade, a campaign that was regarded by many people at the time as an eccentric act of benevolence at best. Although many millions around the world have heard about the Command received by Dr King (described in Chapter 2) through the media, the internet, and various publications, it is not yet one of the central occurrences of our age as, in my view, it should be. For this is the most significant extraterrestrial encounter in modern history.

A bold statement? Certainly. The validation lies not so much in evidence, although I feel the two Russian atomic accidents alone provide this, but more in the quality of the knowledge and the world-saving plan that flowed from that extraordinary happening in May 1954, when Dr King was told of his future role by a cosmic being. Dr King did not at that time have any particular interest in flying saucers. His field was yoga, healing, and spiritual practices of various kinds. So the event that took place was not only a startling surprise, but a completely new direction for him to take. Great events and initiations have been described in mystical and religious writings through the ages, but it is somehow harder for people to accept them when they happen in the most familiar of surroundings—a small apartment in London in the twentieth century—and to a man who could so easily be regarded as just another cranky claimant. I would not blame anyone for questioning the veracity of such an account. I must say that, after careful examination, I too have rejected many claims, but in this case I am fortunate. I knew Dr King well and I know from personal experience that he was exactly what he claimed to be.

Shortly after that life-changing encounter, he received a letter from a school of yoga in London, as had been predicted, attended classes, and learned exercises, especially in pranayama, that prepared him even more than his previous years of practice for the role he was to play. He learned to tune in and receive communications telepathically from the Cosmic Master who had issued the command, the Master Aetherius, and other interplanetary communicators. His role was not to be the world's most convincing and well-versed expert on flying saucers—others performed that function. Dr King's role was to deliver the spiritual aspect of the extraterrestrial message and the cosmic plan for our world. His task became a mission that expanded exponentially.

The method of communication used by Dr King to receive the extraterrestrial messages is known as samadhic trance. In the ancient aphorisms of Sri Patanjali, who is generally regarded as the father of raja yoga, samadhi is the pinnacle of attainment in which the meditator becomes one with that which is beyond even mind. It is a state of soul consciousness—the essence of the meditator's spiritual self radiates through every level of his or her being. Dr King did not use this state in order to bathe in a blissfulness that surpasses all other known forms of joy, a oneness with all life, referred to in many writings in glowing phraseology as the most ineffable of all experiences. He used it for an even higher, and far more selfless, purpose than that. He entered samadhic trance in order to gain rapport with cosmic beings who are on a vastly higher level than we are, and deliver their teachings to Earth.

In this state, which was consciously induced on every occasion and under his complete control, a beam of thought could be radiated to him and translated by his brain into words. Had he been German or French, his brain would have translated the messages into those languages, but because he was from England, the cosmic transmissions were in English. The words came through his mouth and were tape-recorded. Some of them were later transcribed, encapsulating a wealth of teaching, philosophy, and scientific revelation. Great truths were delivered to this world and have been carefully stored in vaults in America and England for posterity. A selection of these appears in Chapter 9 and you can form your own conclusions about their quality and significance.

On occasions, Dr King used another method of receiving transmissions, as referred to in relation to the Chernobyl disaster. These messages were termed mental as opposed to cosmic transmissions. For these, he did not enter a deep samadhic trance state, but was able telepathically to receive the words transmitted to him by cosmic intelligences and then either write them down or record them in his own spoken voice onto a tape recorder. While the cosmic transmissions have a timeless and dramatic impact because of the different voices expressed through his larynx, the mental transmissions do not have this. In the cosmic transmissions, you can hear the voice of a particular cosmic communicator unchanged over decades. It would, in my view, be impossible for an actor to duplicate such a feat so accurately, and Dr King was not a trained actor or voice artist of any kind. Some of the voices have an indescribable beauty to them, others a resonant or sonorous tone, and still others a quaint accent modeled on a terrestrial pattern. In listening to these on tape or CD, you have the benefit not just of the information, but of hearing the inflection and feeling behind the thoughts as they were delivered by the individual communicator.

The mental transmissions were much easier for Dr King to receive, and safer, too. I have seen him receiving a mental transmission on more than one occasion, and regarded it as a great privilege to have been in the same room while he was in contact with an extraterrestrial being. I can vouch for the authenticity of this profound experience. Others have been present during the reception of cosmic transmissions—in fact, in the early days, hundreds thronged the Caxton Hall in Westminster, London, and venues in America and other parts of the world, as he received them "live." One of the unusual features of some of these early cosmic transmissions delivered in public was to give forecasts of when flying saucer activity was due to take place. Confirmation of such activity on those dates came from people from all walks of life, thus proving the identity and existence of these interplanetary communicators. The following is just one example of the numerous forecasts that were confirmed.

"Flying Saucers will be operating on July 7th, 8th, and 9th, generally over the Antipodes. I feel that the vehicles you call Mother Ships should be seen over Australia and New Zealand during that time."

That forecast was made by the Master Aetherius at Caxton Hall on June 30 1956. It was confirmed as follows:

The *Sunday Telegraph*—Sydney, July 8 1956

R.A.A.F. in "Saucer" hunt over Sydney

An R.A.A.F. plane flew over North Sydney yesterday to investigate a report of two different unidentified objects in the air. The pilot found no explanation for the sighting of the objects. The R.A.A.F. was acting on a report from Mr Alan Light of Lloyd Avenue, Cremorne.

Mr Light had earlier told the *Sunday Telegraph* that he and other Cremorne residents sighted two unusual objects in the sky. Mr Light was a radar equipment operator with the R.A.A.F. in World War Two.

"The objects had a metallic appearance and gave off a bright light," he said. "They appeared between noon and 1:00 p.m. about 2,000 feet up. They were almost stationary. The objects disappeared for about an hour, but one re-appeared again about ten past two. They weren't aircraft, nor were they weather balloons. I've seen plenty of them."

Dr King's life was not to be just, or even mainly, about teaching. From the word go, he became not only a channel for the Cosmic Masters but also their agent. He embarked upon a series of missions for the benefit of the planet as a whole under their direction, and even in some cases instigated, with their permission, by himself.

When William Blake wrote that "great things are done when men and mountains meet," he could have been giving a foretaste of one of the early missions that were performed by Dr King on behalf of the Cosmic Masters. This particular mission was called Operation Starlight and took place between July 23 1958 and August 23 1961. This world-changing mission called upon Dr King's physical strength as well as his spiritual abilities, for he was required to act as the channel through which cosmic energies would be placed into selected mountains around the world, providing humanity with an inexhaustible source of spiritual power through these New-Age batteries.

Over the three years and one month it took Dr King and his very small dedicated team of inexperienced climbers to complete this mission, the following mountains were duly charged with cosmic energies:

British Isles
Holdstone Down, Brown Willy, Ben Hope, Creag-An-Leth-Chain, the Old Man of Coniston, Pen-Y-Fan, Carnedd Llywelyn, Kinderscout, and Yes Tor

USA
Mount Baldy, Mount Tallac, Mount Adams, and Castle Peak

Australia
Mount Kosciusko and Mount Ramshead

New Zealand
Mount Wakefield

Tanzania
Mount Kilimanjaro

Switzerland
Mount Madrigerfluh

France
Le Nid D'Aigle

Taking into account its location, height, and the difficulties it posed, Mount Kilimanjaro was charged by members of the Spiritual Hierarchy of Earth without Dr King having to climb it and act as the channel. Even so, it was a truly incredible achievement by one man, giving of himself totally so that he could be used as the channel for eighteen of the nineteen holy mountains to be charged. By praying at the summit of these holy mountains, anyone who wants to can send out tremendous streams of energy to the world. It was during this mission that Dr King moved his base from London, where The Aetherius Society had been founded in 1955, to Los Angeles, where it was incorporated on November 22 1960 as a nonprofit-making organization. The Society continued actively in the British Isles, as it still does today, but was expanding to other parts of the world.

Dr King also performed missions over water. The first of these, Operation Bluewater, took place at sea off Newport Beach, California, a psychic center of the Mother Earth. Its purpose was to bring about a balance of spiritual energies, which had been upset by the wrong thought and action of humanity. This entailed the invention of specialized radionic equipment, which was needed to conduct the vital energies sent by the Cosmic Masters into the psychic center. Not only did Dr King have to design the equipment, he also had to get it built and working perfectly, which was far from straightforward. Once this was accomplished, his skills as a medium were essential in the performance of the mission's four phases, which took place from July 11 1963 to November 29 1964. At sea, Dr King handled the boat for certain maneuvers, while remaining in constant mental contact with the cosmic intelligences who were relaying the navigational patterns to him.

In the meantime, Dr King had developed equipment for use in cooperation with Satellite Number 3. He had been receiving details of this giant spacecraft's regular orbits of the Earth since his early contacts with extraterrestrial beings. The first given orbit started on May 28 1955. Under the control of a Cosmic Master known as Mars Sector 6, the spacecraft radiates specialized energies that enhance the karmic power of all spiritual action. During such periods, referred to as spiritual pushes, all selfless work performed in service to others is made more effective by a factor of three thousand. This does not necessarily mean that if you give healing to someone, they get better three thousand times faster, but it does mean that any spiritual action helps the karma of the world three thousand times more than it would normally. Anyone, irrespective of color, class, or creed, can tune in to these great powers, which are readily available to all who call upon them. You don't have to be associated with The Aetherius Society, or even believe that Satellite Number 3 exists, in order to take advantage of the wonderful energies that are waiting to be used. All you need is the desire to help relieve the suffering of others.

This floating Temple of Light comes into orbit four times every year, from midnight to midnight GMT, on April 18–May 23, July 5–August 5, September 3–October 9, and November 4 –December 10. Many people have commented on the distinct difference they notice when performing spiritual practices during a spiritual push, and the extra power they feel during these special times.

In conjunction with equipment to receive the energies of a spiritual push, Dr King devised what is now known as a spiritual energy radiator, to be run both in England and later in America. This is the apparatus operated so successfully during the Chernobyl disaster. Today, there are five spiritual energy radiators: two in the UK, in London and Barnsley; two in the USA, in Los Angeles and Michigan; and one in New Zealand, in Auckland.

Direct cooperation with Satellite Number 3 still continues even though nobody has, or will, replace Dr King as the communications channel. Although Dr King never claimed to travel physically in an extraterrestrial spacecraft, he did so in a projected, out-of-body state on several occasions. One of these, to Satellite Number 3, is described below in his own words:

At one time I was hovering within my body in deep Meditation, listening in supreme ecstatic bliss to the Creative Voice and in the next moment, like a blinding flash—glorious freedom.

For a moment, I hovered there, within the room, regarding my pitiful body, now slumped forward in the chair, unbreathing, immobile, going cold. The next moment, I was above the city and in a twinkling, I hovered 1,550 miles in Space before a massive object.

From the outside the Third Satellite looks like an enormous egg. I made an estimation of its size to be at least a mile and a half long. Before me, around that floating Temple there was an impenetrable force screen. Yet, even as I neared the Satellite, I detected a movement within this screen. Forces seemed to whirl around and in the middle of the greenish glow of the screen an opening appeared which seemed like a bluish coloured tunnel through which I made my way. A door slid open and closed silently behind me.

I was inside the Third Satellite.

I became immediately aware that I was in a huge room, housing a tremendous amount of beautifully designed apparatus. The whole place was filled with a soft, exquisite radiance, more beautiful than that found in any place on Earth. The atmosphere was filled with an alluring perfume, not strong enough to be detected by the physical senses, but denotable by the reaction it had upon my etheric body. This perfume was an energy which, if concentrated upon, would bring on the deeper states of trance, regarded on Earth as Samadhi. Even though I did not really concentrate upon or tune into this perfume energy, its presence had a clearing effect upon my mind. In the middle

146

of the ceiling, covering about a quarter of its huge domed surface, there was a large circular window. This was made of pure crystal, very finely ground and completely free from all flaws such as those which might be found in terrestrial glass, which would be likely to blur the images seen through it. The crystal window allowed the free passage of all Solar rays as well as magnetic rays coming from other Planetary Bodies, which latter shone against the purple background of Space with a scintillating brilliance never observed from the surface of Earth. The huge crystal window could be made into a filter by charging it with certain energies, affecting its selection of Solar and magnetic rays. During this charging process, the crystal changed colour from a soft rose pink, to a pulsating violet, according to the selection imposed by the Operators of the Satellite. Beneath the huge window stood three large crystal prisms which broke up the Solar spectrum into its primary colours. Each spectromatic colour was then split into seven further shades by another large crystal which held my fascinated gaze. This huge crystal structure seemed to be about 25 to 30 feet high, shaped like a giant egg. What its physical weight must have been, I do not know—but it defied all the known laws of gravity, because it floated in Space, being neither fastened to the domed ceiling or to the metal floor of the Spacecraft. Slowly revolving around this great egg-shaped crystal were numerous other multi-shaped crystalline formations. These moved in slow procession from the top to the bottom in an elliptical orbit. They passed between the tip of the ovoid and the great domed roof of the Spacecraft to continue their travel down the side of it, passing between the bright metal floor and the bottom of this gigantic egg. The great ovoid glowed as from some internal fires; obviously radiating energies which were conditioned by "something" within it.

The primary colours of the Solar rays, broken down by the three huge prisms, were absorbed into the ovoid structure and radiated outwards, each one split up again into seven further aspects of energy. These colours I could not name, because I have never seen their equivalent on Earth. But, I did notice, with great interest, that when each primary colour was broken down by the ovoid, the resultant energy seemed to flow slowly like a kind of liquid capable of being guided through the transmitting mechanism. The latter was made of a type of metal unknown to me, in the shape of a large matrix. This matrix was formed of intricate lines of metal which ran in very finely cut channels intersecting each other at exactly 90 degree angles. In fact, I was later informed that this angle of intersection was computed so exactly that the whole matrix had to be built in Space so that the curvature of a Planetary mass would not affect the precise angles of the intersection! From this matrix the conditioned energies were radiated to any destination on Earth.

The amazing scientists on the Third Satellite have, by a simple process of light manipulation, isolated the Universal Life Forces referred to by the Sages as—Prana. These subtle Pranas are the energies with which the Manipulators on the Third Satellite are flooding this dark little Planet during every "Magnetization Period". They can blend and interweave them in complicated patterns and guide the resultant energies to any spot on the surface of Earth.

This excerpt from the book *The Nine Freedoms* takes the concept of an out-of-body experience to an entirely different level as well as giving a superb inside view of an extraterrestrial spacecraft.

Other missions still continue, over water and inland, the most public of these being Operation Prayer Power. Since this mission started on Holdstone Down in North Devon, England, on June 30 1973, it has been featured dozens of times on television around the world. In January 2010, for example, it was featured on the BBC3 TV documentary "I Believe in UFOs," which included coverage of a pilgrimage to Holdstone Down on July 25 2009. The event was attended by 146 people, some of whom were new to The Aetherius Society.

Dr King combined his hard-earned skills as a master of yoga with his skill as an inventor of radionic equipment to devise Operation Prayer Power. Knowing the power of prayer, and the fact that it is every bit as real an energy as electricity, Dr King invented a way to harness and store it in a physical container, or battery, made of certain materials. This power could then be released to bring aid and relief following the cataclysmic effects of hurricanes, earthquakes, tsunamis, forest fires, and other such disasters. As we all know, at a time of crisis it is difficult to gather a large group of people to pray together and send out healing to a stricken area. Operation Prayer Power provides the answer because the stored energy can be released at short notice as and when it is needed. Anyone who believes in the power of prayer can contribute—all that is needed is the desire to be of service to others.

People gather together regularly and by chanting mantras, an effective way of invoking spiritual energy, they focus their concentration on directing the energy to someone who is praying in front of the battery. The prayers used are those contained in *The Twelve Blessings*, which were channeled by the Master Jesus through Dr King. The battery can hold several hundred hours of prayer energy, which can be released when needed to help disaster victims, or to aid relief workers. It can also be of great help when directed to important peace talks. Energy is released from the battery through a spiritual energy radiator, and then manipulated by the Cosmic Masters to bring the greatest possible benefit to the world. The decision about where the energy is to be sent is made by a small number of highly experienced officers of The Aetherius Society, who, through specialized training and instruction, are able to communicate the request to the Cosmic Masters, although no individual is qualified or authorized to receive a response. This method of one-way communication was established by Dr King to insure that certain missions could continue after his passing. Missions, including Operation Sunbeam and the Saturn Mission, which were performed by Dr King in his lifetime, have also continued to be performed since his demise.

Dr King's work in cooperation with the Cosmic Masters extended beyond the physical to other levels of this Earth, both higher and especially lower. In the latter case, this involved receiving transmissions about battles between the forces of light and the forces of darkness, always for the betterment of humanity as a whole. They say that as above so below, but in this case it was a matter of preventing the below affecting the above. Surpassing even the most vivid description of perhaps Europe's greatest ever poet, Dante, whose *Inferno* is believed by some to be more than just a fictional portrayal, these accounts show that Cosmic Beings will go into the deepest and darkest places if they are permitted to do so in order to bring hope and light to those regions and thereby to the world as a whole.

One of the great revelations given by the Cosmic Masters is that many, though not all, of our most famous spiritual teachers through history have been from other worlds. Those who came to help and teach us, at different times and in different ways, include the Lord Buddha, the Master Jesus, Sri Krishna, Lao-Tse, Confucius, Sri Patanjali, Sri Sankaracharya, Sri Ramakrishna, Moses, and Samson. Unlike the Cosmic Masters, who have spacecraft and both technological and spiritual powers at their disposal, these were interplanetary beings who chose to be incarnated in our world and so were subject to earthly limitations, accepting that karma in order to serve humanity. Among the most terrible of all these karmic burdens was the dreadful death of the Master Jesus, which, I believe, should not be celebrated as a passion but regarded with remorse and shame as well as the most profound gratitude.

Dr King brought a deeper understanding of karma and its workings, in my view, than has ever been brought to Earth before. He understood karma not as a theoretical, philosophical concept, which happens rather vaguely over many lifetimes, but as a living, vivid force that operates twenty-four hours a day. He described it as "pressure toward conformity." This idea of karma, in almost scientific terms, as pressure is new and, on the face of it, challenging. Yet, when properly understood, it is liberating, because this is a pressure we should not fight, resist, or try to avoid as we might do with so-called "stress-busting techniques." That won't work with karma. It is a force we should accept. Only through accepting and acting in the light of it will we find our own enlightenment. The key action that we need to take is service to the whole, not just to our family and friends, much as we are responsible to them, but to the whole human race, and even the planet, the Mother Earth, as the living being that she is.

The following words were written by Brian Keneipp, who is executive secretary of The Aetherius Society in America, and has been a good friend of mine for many years. He was a very close follower of Dr King, especially during the latter period of his life. In particular, he has had a prominent role in the preservation and propagation of the transmissions, both during Dr King's lifetime and since his death.

In order to understand the transmissions given to Earth through Dr King, I think it may be helpful to look briefly through my eyes at Dr King during the time he was receiving these channeled messages.

I had the privilege to have been on Dr King's personal staff in Los Angeles from 1978 to his passing. This period of time was indeed an amazing experience. I was especially close to him in the last years of his life when I was one of his close advisors and healers from 1987 to his passing in 1997. During that period, I was with him and on call 24 hours a day 7 days a week. I lived in the same house, or in an adjacent one, for all of these years. Having this much access to him, and watching him deal with others, I learned firsthand many things about him. First and foremost was that he was absolutely focused on helping the world. Never would a day pass but that he would be thinking of, and acting in, ways to help the world. This could manifest in many ways, from communicating the schedule of operations of Satellite Number 3 around Earth for the future, to arranging spiritual energy to be given on behalf of humanity to the Mother Earth, to transferring a mission he designed to the Spiritual Hierarchy of Earth. A mission to help release energy from the Mother Earth to the devic kingdom will help usher in the New Age (as described in my book *Operation Earth Light* published by Aetherius Press).

He rarely took days off—but he did enjoy himself and had many laughs with those around him. He was kind and generous with an active sense of humor. Yet he also expected those around him always to do their best—and he had a way of knowing what your best was. He could be very hard on those around him, as he was often pushing us to achieve this, both in what we did for him and everything else.

This may sound similar to the stories of disciples in the East living with a Master. However, there were major differences. For one thing he was not so focused on living the role of a personal Master. His focus was more to help the world evolve and to help others help the world evolve.

Big difference.

When people who knew of Dr King's work discovered how close I was with him, they would often say, "How lucky you were, you must have been able to talk with him about so many things and be guided by him."

Well, yes and no.

Yes, I was fortunate and was able to learn much by observing him and having him push and guide me in many ways. But he rarely advised on spiritual practices or discussed the goings on beyond Earth privately. He remained focused on creating a spiritual brotherhood that would be able to continue to cooperate with the Cosmic Masters after he passed on.

Living in Dr King's residence as one of his personal assistants, I was constantly aware of the big picture of the position of our civilization on Earth. Ours is a backward and virtually barbaric race—still in the habit of killing each other, still in the dark about our very nature and the nature around us. It became very real that there are many worlds beyond our planet, even in this solar system, which are much more evolved both spiritually and scientifically than we are. And though they are desperate to help us, their hands are tied due to the law of karma. They can only help in certain ways at this time. In fact, Dr King and the Cosmic Masters spent much of their time stretching and working the law of karma to help mankind as much as they possibly could. This thread is seen throughout the transmissions themselves.

He was in close contact with the Cosmic Masters. Rarely would more than a couple of days go by when he would not have some form of contact with advanced beings. Many of these contacts were not recorded, for many reasons. Needless to say, Dr King was involved with many things beyond the norm. Being with him so closely during this time, I observed many of these unrecorded communications as well as the recorded ones. These communications, Dr King's life and actions, and his guidance to those around him all reinforced one central theme: Service to others and thankfulness to God. The more these two types of thoughts or vibrations replace humanity's normal thoughts and vibrations of selfishness and self-centeredness, the more mankind will evolve and the more we can be helped. As we receive more help we will be inspired to increase our selfless deeds and thoughts—and so the spiral upward can continue.

Dr King was a master of karma yoga. He was always looking for ways to leverage this spiral. He was always looking for ways to get the pressure of karma to push mankind forward quicker. This brings me back to how different it was living with Dr King. It was evident almost every day that Dr King was not acting alone. He was not like the classic eastern master with one main task to help his many disciples evolve individually. No. Dr King was virtually a karmic agent on Earth. His mission was to speed up this cycle of our evolution from selfishness to selflessness. He was being used by greater Masters to bring through profound wisdom needed on Earth at this time, such as The Twelve Blessings and The Nine Freedoms. He was also finding ways that ordinary people like me, coming together with other normal individuals, could cooperate with advanced masters on behalf of mankind, to help speed up humanity's evolution. At times Dr King would request and receive help from outside sources on missions he was engaged in himself for humanity. For example, many times he arranged for valuable help during natural catastrophes, such as floods, hurricanes, or fires, that were threatening thousands of people. We have documented several amazing instances where virtual miracles were achieved. Dr King was able to gain the cooperation of the Cosmic Masters and aspects of the Spiritual Hierarchy of Earth to relieve suffering. He accomplished this by getting us more ordinary individuals to put forth focused and precisely timed effort to act as a karmic trigger to allow greater beings to come in to help. Their help manifested in the form of great spiritual energy being flooded to the affected region, which would give those helping on the spot tremendous strength, ability, and inspiration.

Although most of the transmissions received by Dr King can be partially understood alone, when you piece them together amidst the over one thousand transmissions he received, and in the context of Dr King's life, they represent an amazing whole—a whole that is much more than a philosophy; a whole that is designed to inspire one to ACTION. For this is the main message. Mankind needs to change. To do so we must act in service to others. We must move from selfishness to selflessness. And the speed of this change needs to increase. It is a challenge to get across the essence of these thousand-plus transmissions to those who read them, but do not hear them. There is a big difference.

Most of the public cosmic transmissions given up to 1981 were recorded on very high-quality equipment. When you hear a transmission you can hear not only the words but the tone, the inflexion, and the timing as given by the Cosmic Masters. Even more, you are able to feel the vibration of the voice—and that can be an amazing experience to say the least. I can say this from personal experience. Over the last several years I have overseen the transfer of all of the cosmic transmissions from reel to reel analog tape to high-resolution digital sound files. I have also had a hand in the re-mastering of several of the key transmissions. The more I heard these beautiful transmissions the more moved I was by not only the words but the powerful essence behind the words. Some of these are available from The Aetherius Society in audio form and, as the years go by, more will become so.

Even the later mental transmissions, many of which I recorded and transcribed at the time they were received, have an essence to them beyond the words themselves.

Still the words themselves can have an amazing impact upon one who is ready and open to their vibration. I ask you to be skeptical, as one should with any new source of wisdom, but also to be open. This is information that has been given to mankind from outside our world to help us all wherever we are and whatever we believe.

CHAPTER 9

The extra-terrestrial message

Serve and be great! Nay—be everlasting.

Mars Sector 6

I n a television interview in the 1970s in England, Dr King made the following statements when questioned about his cosmic contacts:

I've had very, very regular contacts. I've had hundreds of transmissions about various things, some of them are of a very scientific nature and I have physically met people that live on other worlds ...

They're very advanced people, scientifically and spiritually, philosophically very much our superiors. They would have to be in order to travel through space as they do, because they not only travel through this solar system but go outside of this solar system to other parts of the galaxy and even outside of this galaxy to other galaxies, feats which we can only dream about at this present time. They can materialize, or dematerialize, at will—in other words appear in various places—they can take on other forms, they can project their consciousness, they can project their thoughts, so they are very much superior to us ...

To condemn is easy; to investigate is much more difficult, but much more profitable ...

I would like to say something else too, you know. These messages were given, we do have them down on tape, they have been published. Well, from the philosophical content alone, they are pretty fantastic—so they did come from somewhere. Either they came from my mind or they came from another source. If they came from another source, they're excellent. If they came from my puny little mind, then I'm quite a person.

In his typically understated way, Dr King illustrated in this interview the key point about the cosmic and mental transmissions he had received. They could either be genuinely received from extraterrestrial intelligences as he claimed, or be an invention of his own. He did not claim to be capable of delivering such wisdom as is contained in these communications, which means it can only have come from the Cosmic Masters. I would go further than Dr King, in his modesty, was willing to do. The originator of these transmissions could not have been either a conman or a self-deluded individual. The very nature of them evokes profundity, purity, and compassion in their every inflection. A deluded or deluding individual would not be capable of generating such incomparable works as these.

I once came across an article by a literary critic about William Blake, and his claim to have used what we would now call channeling in some of his work. The critic proceeded to explain that Blake must have suffered from some form of mental illness, probably schizophrenia, to believe such a thing, but also praised his writing as being among the greatest in poetic literature. In doing so, he was implying that elevated perceptions and insights can be the product of severe mental illness and delusion, a theory that I would dispute. There is a much simpler explanation, namely that some of Blake's work was, just as he said, the result of his clairvoyant and clairaudient experiences with angelic and other higher beings. An honest, clear, and inspired mind produces honest, clear, and inspired thoughts. In the case of Dr King, it was his ability to attain such a refined level of sensibility through his yogic and other spiritual disciplines that prepared him for the advanced communicators who were to use him as their channel.

In the end, though, the only thing that matters is the caliber of the extraterrestrial message itself. The remainder of this chapter consists of extracts from the hundreds of transmissions that were delivered during the forty-three years that Dr King acted as Primary Terrestrial Mental Channel. I am grateful to Brian Keneipp for making this carefully ordered selection of fourteen priceless gems from the cornucopia of riches that is Dr King's unique, mediumistic legacy. I am also grateful to the international directors of The Aetherius Society for giving permission for these to be published.

The first extract is the answer to a two-part question that was posed to the Master Aetherius: "Can you give us a little about the comparative chemistry of the physical bodies used on Venus? Is there any comparison with our chemistry of carbon compounds, for instance?"

The Master Aetherius, October 25 1954

It is rather complicated because a lot of us exist in subtle states and when we come to this Planet, or to Mars, or any other World, we build for ourselves a body to live on that Planet. If the people of that particular Planet have twenty-seven legs, as some people have in the Milky Way, then we can build a body with these twenty-seven legs. If carbon is the basic cellular property, we can use this by drawing it out of the atmosphere and blending it in such a way as to form a cellular structure, in harmony with environmental conditions prevalent upon that particular Planet we are visiting. On the other hand, we can use a silicon base; certain plants have a silicon base. There are few people on Venus who use bodies of a coarser matter and these only when necessary—yet we are physical beings.

It is not possible for me to give English names, for the constituents of the molecules of the subtle bodies, because you have no words to describe them. So tenuous are these bodies, that it would be like giving a name to the molecules of your Soul, as it were. It would be impossible to do that, unless you had a language like certain of the Planets with 25,000 symbols in the alphabet. That language is never written.

The Master Aetherius, January 29 1955—Extract 1

I will say a word about our religion. It is simplicity. We believe in one God, all is one, although one part may disturb another part and the resultant disturbance causes an appearance of disunity. If you think about it you will see that it is because of the unity of the whole system that one part can disturb another part. The fact that if you steal of your brother, that ritual affects a man in China, we accepted many years ago and we have based the whole of our philosophy, our religion, upon this definite law of oneness. That is why, don't you see, we must be interested in your little Bikini tea parties. [The Master Aetherius is referring to the numerous atomic bomb tests performed near the Bikini Islands in the 1950s.] You not only affect your own system but you are definitely beyond any doubt affecting ours as well. The whole planetary system, my friends, is one family linked together with very strong magnetic links, which has come from a common womb, that of the Sun, one family that feels strongly for the rest of its relations. So our religion takes this into account, this oneness, this simplicity.

Very few know what it means "Be still and know that I Am God", and yet although it is a very simple statement, it is one of the greatest in the Interplanetary System. So when I say our religion is simple, I do not mean that the young people would find it simple I mean that it is religion or a belief that recognizes reality is unchangeability—your own worthy Masters say just the same thing. We are trying to make you realize that your own Masters on Terra [this Latin word is often used by the Cosmic Masters for Earth] have told you the way, but you have strayed from that way. All my talk has been said before, hundreds of times, on your very world. There is not anything new. If there were one thing new it would mean the Absolute had not put that thing there in the beginning, that is why there can be nothing new. There can be a modern presentation, but that modern presentation is just a 1955 label for something trillions of years old. The Ancient Wisdom was written in the beginning by the Hand of the Absolute Architect of the palatial system. Our religion is not anything new but what yours should be; our education is not anything new, but what yours should be; our political system is not anything new, but what yours should be.

Our belief in an Absolute Architect, an Absolute Creator, thinking into being certain laws which are immutable, these are the things we study first; secondly we apply these laws to our political system and our educational system. We do not try to get the laws to fit in with our preconceived ideas of what things should be, we make our systems fit the law. When you do that, you will become luminous in the heavens, you will immediately go one step further upwards, you will immediately be showered by Flying Saucers and Mother Ships, call them what you like, who will come from planets to walk your Earth. But they will not come in great numbers like that until you have gone forward to make your present system subservient to the Law of God. It seems very strange that thousands of years ago most of the beings upon Terra did that, and then started the great system of involution, the great drop into sin, and now you are starting on the way back, a way back that will be hard, a way back that will be difficult. It will be very easy for some of you to say, "that fellow was talking about things that Mr So and So should do something about but not myself." I am talking to you in this way because all of you can do something about these things. If you will raise your consciousness a little bit, you will raise the consciousness of the whole world a little bit. A grave responsibility lies upon the shoulders of all of you; you can reject it or act upon it.

The Master Aetherius, January 29 1955—Extract 2

We of the Interplanetary Government System have been interested in Terra for some generations. This interest has been quickened by atom studies and nearness to space travel. Within a couple of years from today you should be able to draw up blueprints of your first Space Station and propel this into a predetermined position. Interplanetary governmental system will welcome you providing you come in peace. If the more bloodthirsty among you decide to take a radio controlled projectile on to that space station, you will be violating a law, a law laid down by even greater beings than we are.

We are interested in your world, because you have been marked down as a young planet in the planetary system, a grey planet in the system, and indeed, you are the only planet that is not properly represented in the Interplanetary Parliament, the seat of which is on Saturn. You see, when once you get outside the surface chaos of your foolish political systems and think about travelling to your solar planets, you enter a field or an area of comparative harmony. Certainly harmony if you were to compare it with your worldly chaos. Now that harmony has taken many trillions of years to fabricate, and it would not be in the best interests to encourage one who is liable to upset that harmony to enter into the area where that harmony exists.

So we are offering the hand of friendship because we wish to advise you so that your scientists may prepare themselves, your politicians may prepare themselves and your religious leaders may prepare themselves for journeys to the planets, and your consciousness will be broadened greatly by such a journey. The whole consciousness of your world will be risen when man can return with so-called factual reports of the conditions now existing on other planets. He will see how wrong their academic scientists were when they said that such and such a planet is not capable of holding a life form which is anything near to the human. There are many life forms in the planets more human, if I may use the term in the broadest sense, than most of the people in your world.

The Master Aetherius, July 28 1956

This mind has a soul or controller—the soul not being the Spirit, of course—this soul has brought around itself other magnetic forces and moulded them into a cellular structure which gives the appearance of being solid—it is most certainly not—and the whole can walk about, jump about and so on. It is really and truly magnetism held in a certain state—we call it solidified light. Where does the light come from? It comes from the Sun; so, therefore, whether you like it or not, your bodies are, and indeed every other thing on this particular planet is, solidified sunlight ... It was created by the Divine Creator. So, therefore, everything is the original potential brought into manifestation and held in a certain state by the Will of the Divine Creator, and you are apparently—note, I say apparently—individualised units expressing that Will. It is as simple as that.

Please, please try to regard always—try to tell yourself always—that the most unanswerable things have really the simplest answers, and whole new avenues of wisdom will be opened out to you—wisdom that you did not dream you could attract and understand before you adopted this simple and straightforward approach.

The following extract consists of transmissions delivered by two Cosmic Masters through Dr King on November 24 1956.

First Communicator—Mars Sector 6

Subject—A Sign

Many brothers of Terra have requested from us a sign. Many signs have been given by people from other Planets, signs which should have proved to thinking terrestrial men beyond any doubt that we do exist, that we are indeed living entities, that we have indeed the interest of Terra at heart. As numerous, though, as these signs have been, they still do not satisfy certain terrestrial intelligences. I ask my brothers from Terra who require as a sign a landing of one of our craft in a prominent position, to give US a sign!

Science has requested a sign from Flying Saucers. I ask science to give us their sign. What sign do we require? Their goodwill, their complete, open-minded honesty and their proof that if we reveal to them the secrets of the vibrations of crystals, these secrets will be used for the benefit of all. We cannot reveal our science to the scientists of Terra until they prove to us their Godliness. We would only be instrumental in taking Terra back another seventy decades if we gave the secrets of our gravitational control to you now. Would it benefit you? Not so. Would it benefit the ordinary man? It would not. It would be used for belligerent purposes; a belligerence which would be covered by the camouflage of defence. Then, science, know this: When you give unto us a sign, then will we give unto you a sign, the sign which you now require. This will be accepted as the measure of your goodwill.

This Transmission came from Mars Sector 6, with the sanction and authority of Interplanetary Parliament, based upon the Planet Saturn. I will now switch relay through to that Intelligence known to Terra as Aetherius.

Second Communicator—The Master Aetherius

Of course it is so. My friends, it is a pleasure to be able to speak to you again for I see the thought patterns of the majority of you, and I see that you are seekers after Truth. Some have tried many other ways, many other paths to peace, yet have failed to find peace. Dear friends, what is peace? Surely it is something which is above politics, above national interest, above even that thing which you upon Terra call love. Peace, dear friends, is enlightenment. There is only one sin in the whole Cosmic system, that is the sin of ignorance. Please spell that again—enlightenment—and you have peace.

If Terra were enlightened there would be no such thing as a rich man; neither would there be a poor one. There would be no such thing as disease;

there would be no such thing as a King; there would be no such thing as a dictator; there would be no such thing as a Prime Minister; there would be no such thing as money. Hospitals would not be needed. There would be no need for travel even, because on a correctly enlightened Planet, travel between one part of the Planet and another is done so easily by teleportation and thought projection.

Think for a moment about what I have said. Just imagine for a moment, if these conditions were in vogue upon Earth NOW how happy you would all be. You would not need to worry about your family, your old age—infirmity stopping you from working hard for bare subsistence. Not at all would you. Subsistence would be guaranteed to you by all.

Don't you see, dear friends, as my friend from the Planet Mars has already told you, that if your men in power were to have faith in God instead of a moth-eaten, wicked political system—if science were to have faith in metaphysics instead of the binding limitation of common mathematics—if an economic system were more interested in the world as a whole than it is in its own selfish interests, we could then come among you freely, easily. We could then give to you safely our secrets of Interplanetary and Interstellar travel. Yes, Interstellar! We could give to you our secrets of physical transportation by thought from any position upon the surface of your Planet to any other position upon the surface of your Planet. We could allow you then to visit our Planets, to travel for yourselves through the Solar System in the vehicles you call Flying Saucers.

We could safely make these revelations to you but it is a big "IF", isn't it? You will all admit that won't you? Most of you do, anyway.

Do you see, some people upon Terra demand from Planetary Intelligences certain information—information about Lithium 9, information about Tri-helium, information about tuning into and use of existing magnetic fields. This information has been requested from our Agents now living upon Terra, by science. Scientists say: "Give us this information and you then will be able easily to prove yourself." When our Agents reply: "My friend, I cannot trust you with such information," what happens? We are disbelieved, our presence is ignored, our very existence is laughed at by those people who should know better. Now do you see, dear friends, why we cannot reveal these great secrets to you until you reveal to us the manifestation of the Spiritual potentialities of your soul.

Reveal this to us and we will give you everything we have.

Reveal this to us and we will land among you.

If we landed before this great revelation upon your part, we would be breaking the Laws as laid down by The Lords of Karma. If we landed freely among you and gave to you the secrets of projecting thought by light beams and light by thought impulses, you would be able to sit in a room like this and easily conquer the whole Russian army. Five officers of the Russian army would be able to wipe out the American army, and so it would go on—threat upon threat.

No, dear friends, I want to impress upon you that we are not heartless; we know of your grave difficulties, but don't you see that you have those difficulties because somewhere down along the path of evolution you have done things which have brought those difficulties upon yourselves, so you have to find the way out—YOU have to work your way out. Certainly we will help you to do it, but we cannot give you complete help until you make a start—individually and collectively.

Now I wanted to put that straight because I have this past month seen detailed analyses of the thought patterns of many very good terrestrial men and very good terrestrial ladies, and prevalent—although certain of them may have been unconscious of the fact—prevalent in these thought patterns was the question: "If the people from other Planets have our interest at heart, why then are they so backward in coming forward?" I have answered this question fully. It is up to you. Go forward as instructed by your Holy Works, that is all you have to do, you know. You do not have to start working miracles. You just have to get hold of a little book written about Buddha, a little book written about Jesus, a little book written about Sri Krishna, a little book written about Sankaracharya, and study it. That is all you have to do. And study it. Then apply the theory to your mind and act upon it. That is the answer. That is the answer.

These Great Masters I have mentioned were specially trained in the high Cosmic Mystery Schools before They came in sacrifice to Terra. They did not guess at anything at all. They knew exactly—exactly—what They were saying and how to say it and when to say it. They were trained by the Great Cosmic Adepts of Saturn Itself—all of these Masters were—and given high Cosmic Initiation before apparent terrestrial birth. So there was nothing hit or miss about it—it was hit, and hit only. What They said was true, not complete—of course not, nothing can speak complete Truth, it is above sound—but Their Truth was complete enough to put Terra back into the Realms of Light from which She fell.

That is all you have to do. It is ridiculously easy. The answer to all your problems is absurdly simple, whether they be personal problems or Planetary ones. Read the Law; know that the Law is God, and act upon it—nothing else. Yet the heart of my terrestrial brothers is willing, but alas, the flesh is indeed weak. However, I condemn you not, but say this, that the more you help yourselves, the more help will the Masters give to you.

Yes, dear friends, you will be helped to do these things but, please, when people say to you: "Well, why don't the people from other Planets come and give us this, that and the other of a sign?" say: "Well, why don't you give the people from other Planets a sign first?" Their answers will be interesting indeed, I think. If they ask you what sign we need, say to them the things I have told you this evening, or your own version of these facts.

Even though it is so, I personally have given many signs and many of you have been able to see our vessels. However, to do this has now become very much more difficult because of the deterioration in the situation upon Terra, but when this situation eases—as it will if all of you pray hard enough—we will then be able to give you our lists of future activity. This does not infer, of course, that activity is not going on at the moment. It is. Very much of it. But it has been considered policy just for a short time not to reveal this activity or forecast it as I used to.

I would like to give you a reason for this. I will tell you why I am not giving Flying Saucer forecasts just at the moment. It is because the state of affairs in the world has caused certain governments—America, Britain, Russia and so on—to prepare for any attempt at the violation of their skies by each other. It is a most absurd situation, but there you are. Now, if I were openly to say that Flying Saucers would be over North-West London, for argument's sake, as I used to, fighter aircraft would be alerted because the Air Ministries are interested in all the transmissions given in this way. They have their agents at most meetings and have tapped telephone lines and so on, especially in America and places like that. Well then, these alerted aircraft would do no damage at all to us, but they may damage themselves, so I do not want, myself, to run the risk of this. However, when complete analysis of the thought pattern of the military strategists has been examined, we will be able then to see whether future forecasts would be a good thing or not.

So, my friends, I must thank you all for your attention, for your lively attention this evening. Please, though, do not stop at that. Think about the things I have said. Apply them to your consciousness and, if acceptable, act—ACT—ACT!

I must vacate my position. Before I do though, I would like a moment's silence. Close your eyes, look upwards with your eyes closed.

I invoke the Power of the Cosmic Masters from the Sun and Saturn this very moment. May this Power flow through you this very moment so that you may know that God dwells silently within you all.

Bless you, my friends, goodnight.

The Master Aetherius, February 28 1960

My friends, if I knew you were incapable of spending much of your Energy in service of others, I would not even condescend to speak to you. It is because I can see your individual and collective potential,

I speak unto you in this manner. It is service which should be your keynote. You may murder the foul dragon competition, for this will lead you further into involution, further into all manner of foulness and dictatorship than any other thing.

Let us examine for a moment how the dark forces work, then we can tear them out of the cupboard and we will be able to recognize them in future when they come tapping at our doors with—sliminess.

As men live upon Earth, so the great dark forces are in the lower astral realms. Cunning beings who have protected themselves from death as you know it. Beings who want to gain control of the whole Planet.

Neone in infinitely variable pattern. Beam six, six, zero. Transmission state—good, but full protective measures must be given, because of the value of the information factor.

Granted.

Thank you. [This refers to a manipulation that was carried out as a protection for Dr King as the mental channel for this transmission.]

These dark forces wish to gain control of the whole Planet. So what do they do? They bring about those conditions of confusion within the minds of weak-willed Terrestrial man so that fear, the great evil, enters in. Once fear is there, then doubt comes in by the same door, for the door is wide open. This is the state where the great Power that you worship without understanding, lies almost dormant. Then, in this state can man be told very cunningly about the great enjoyments of certain sexual pleasures and the power moves, so that a great yearning is started within man, so that he becomes—"body". In order to satisfy this yearning, man must use the power a little further so that he may become brain and mind, so that he may co-operate further with the foul machine of cunningly conceived materialism. So he educates his mind for two purposes: firstly, to co-operate with the materialistic trap, but secondly, to further indulge in his basic delights. Then the dark forces have him. He is cornered, he is trapped.

167

He imposes limitation after limitation upon himself and life after life he comes back in this foul scheme of limitation.

How do you break this?

You can tear a dark force wide open and break away quite easily by detaching yourself from your basic delights, by detaching yourself from the materialistic scheme of things.

What happens?

You send out fear. You send out doubt by the same door. You become a person of courage. Why? Because you are a person of Light, who has activated the Karmic Law upon your behalf. You have not fallen for the trap of those who devise conditions so that you would activate the Karmic Law against yourself. No, you have activated it positively and its positive rays come down unto you and the great Power moves—but in its entirety, up through the Centres. Your brain and mind become open to the forces latent within you and you become all-powerful and all-knowing.

No longer can they activate conditions against you, for you stand protected in the midst of the battle and your armour, my friends, is not the armour of men, but the armour put around you by The Great Ones, by the Spark of God within yourself and you go forward a virtual Spiritual juggernaut, shedding your Light and casting out fear and doubt whenever it raises its foul head.

The Master Jesus, September 7 1958

Man dwelleth in a world of selfishness—God dwelleth in a world of selfless expansion.

Bridge this gap—and be a GOD.

The Master Aetherius, November 16 1957

You know, you people really are reaching out to try to find your way through what would appear to you, to be a maze.

Yet, dear friends, deep within, you all know that this reaching outward, is but a reflection of that which is within you. Is that mental and physical manifestation of that great hunger for the right kind of Spiritual knowledge which, dear friends, burns within you now.

Reach outwards. Reach upwards but do not ever, My Brothers—please—forget to reach inwards. For although the outside world has much to offer it cannot offer you one small part of what the inside world can offer you.

Do you see, when you—as a point of Super-consciousness—fabricated for yourselves, a psychic, mental and physical body, you included most aspects of the whole Universe in the result of that task.

It is not by any chance that you used atoms to build the molecules, which build the cells, which together constitute your physical structure. It is not by any chance that those self-same atoms which you used in this task, are but tiny reflections of the Solar System. This is not just some coincidence, for coincidence does not now—neither will it ever—exist.

You made your physical, mental and psychic structures but tiny reflections of the Solar System and when you began the task of building these bodies, you—the Super-conscious You—included all the aspects of the Solar System and then brought them into a usable size and shape. This was a planned operation!

Now, dear friends, this is so, as your meditations will tell you beyond all doubt. Because this is so, why travel so far outwards into the world of materialism when the full model of the Solar System is within you?

You know, the shortest journey that you can make takes you the longest time to complete. That, dear friends, is the journey within you.

If you go deep within your own hearts, deep within your own minds, deep within your own intuition and bring forth the treasures as you find them, into the world outside, then, dear friends, can you illustrate to yourselves, that you are really Angels in disguise. You can then illustrate to your younger brothers, that there are more opportune paths down which you can guide their faltering feet.

Mars Sector 6, January 12 1957

I, myself, and Aetherius, and all other planetary communicators who have ever come to Terra over this last 18 million of your Earth years, would rather one of you pray for an enemy, than all of you expend your prayers in our directions. My dear friends, give your love to God. Pray for your enemies. Take up your holy works, and take them inwards to your heart. If you do these things, you will have no enemies—you will have a great peace and a great understanding.

Mars Sector 6, February 22 1961

If you would prepare yourselves for the New World, you would serve.

Service is indeed a glorious undertaking! It is lasting, for every act of Service is written in everlasting letters of fire in the Akashic Book. When you walk into the Halls of self judgment, you will read what your own hand hath written upon these pages and by the immutable Law of Karma, you will accordingly set limitation upon your rebirth.

Break away from your own troubles by concentrating upon the sufferings of others.

Serve in the great Spiritual battle and you can walk with head high and stand in any Hall unafraid to read what be written there.

The greatest Yoga is—Service.

The greatest Religion is—Service.

The greatest act is that act done in—Service.

Kill possession. Transmute selfishness into Service for others and your reward will come. Enlightenment, like the break of dawn upon the darkest night, will cast the shadows of this night before it.

Serve—and you will become Enlightened.

Serve—and you will be practising true selfless Love.

Serve—and the mighty Power of Kundalini will rise in natural, unforced fashion and open the Chakra jewels in your higher bodies, in will pour inspiration and you will be standing on the verge of the Initiation into Adeptship.

There are no words great enough to describe the wonder of—Service.

And no words can describe the crime of selfishness.

Know this. Whether you like it or not does not matter, it is the Truth. I, Mars, do declare it as such. If you believe it not today, terrestrial man, you will know it in your morrow.

Mars Sector 6, September 15 1956

This is Mars Sector 6 reporting.

Subject—The Conspiracy.

There are more of our vehicles being seen at the moment around Terra than ever before, and yet fewer reports are reaching the press. This is because of a conspiracy to deny our existence. Dear friends, do not let the conspirators be successful. Were it not that there are thousands of our vehicles at this very moment screening Terra, you would not live to walk from this room. This, irrespective of what your official sources tell you. There are more sightings by professional and amateur spotters now than ever before, and yet only a few are ever made known.

You talk upon Terra about the Silence Group. It does exist. The Silence Group—what is it? I will tell you beyond doubt. It is run by the great financial organizations—organizations that move countries—organizations which cause conflict between one country and another, so that war may result. So that their profit may be great indeed. Organizations which have sworn to rule Terra with an iron hand. They cannot do it openly. How can they do it? There is only one way. That is by playing one faction off against another and causing internal strife between the two.

The Silence Group does exist.

It is like some insidious monster in your midst, working by day and night.

The Mental Channel that I use at the moment was approached and his permission gained before these statements were made public, because of the danger in which he would be. However, he, like ourselves, saw fit that the revelation of this knowledge should take place.

The dark forces upon your Earth are highly organized. It is the Forces of Light which are not organized by the ordinary man. One religious body is at loggerheads with another, and yet all black magic ritual [this refers to negative magical practices and has nothing to do with race] is synchronized so that a predetermined and specific result may be brought about. Your religions are split. Where is the synchronization? It does not exist. You have certain religious factors saying to the congregation, "You may not attend any other church". You have other religious factors saying that their sister religions are useless because they only believe so and so and not this and that. Where is the synchronization there? It does not exist. Yet all the time the insidious monster is working among you, fostering this mental break, fostering this psychic break between religion and religion.

The most difficult people upon Earth for us to approach, either directly or indirectly by impression, are some of the most ardent churchgoers. We are not inferring that there is anything wrong with this going to church—it is a wonderful thing—but please, we would ask you people who do so to try to bring about an understanding in your church with all the other churches. Walk in front of a Master and He will tell you beyond doubt that you must study the whole of philosophy to know anything about a part of it. Certain Masters upon Earth are saying this at this moment, and yet certain so-called teachers in the West will not have anything to do, from an official point of view, with Eastern thought and philosophy. Don't you see, that is the break? Don't you see why these things are going on? The insidious monster works slowly, coolly and with calculation, to bring about the result of terrestrial dictatorship.

Spiritual Power—and that only—can stop the workings of this foul octopus in your midst.

Yes, certainly, certain factors from Mars and Venus wish to speak, not only to the people of Los Angeles but to the people of London and the people of New York, to the people of Sydney, to the people of Moscow, but we know that at the moment the authorities would turn our request down. People say to us, "If they turn your request down, then flood their broadcasting circuits with your message". We can do this quite easily from one hundred thousand miles away—nay, we can do this from Mars Itself—stop all radio signals within two minutes, but it would not be right to use such force. My friend Aetherius has told you that if you give a starving man a lot of food and he eats it at once, it will cause him grievous harm. We can, however, introduce that food a little at a time. We are doing this at the moment, very gently and subtly in certain ways, openly in others.

This, then, is the gist of my message. If they say the Spacecraft have gone, smile friends, with tolerance. If you do not see your papers filled with reports, know that "unofficial" officialdom has kept those reports from the press. We are here among you. We will remain among you as long as you need us.

This is Mars relaying to Terra through Primary Mental Channel, with the sanction and authority of Interplanetary Parliament ... now out.

The following mental transmission was addressed to Dr King by the Lord Babaji, the most prominent member of the Spiritual Hierarchy of Earth. Dr King is being informed of the official start of a highly specialized mission called Operation Earth Light, and being thanked for giving the design for this mission to the Spiritual Hierarchy. Dr King realized that The Aetherius Society was not in a position to perform it and decided to offer it to the Spiritual Hierarchy. Operation Earth Light is designed to help usher in the New Age by releasing certain energies from the Earth to the nature spirits known as the devic kingdom.

The Lord Babaji, November 10 1990

On November 11th, 1990, three Units of Operation Earth Light will be activated and remain on the air for several days. We will inform you when these are taken off the air.

Position of these Units is strictly classified; however, it can be announced that these Units will be put on the air on November 11th, 1990.

We wish to thank you for your Operation Earth Light. This Mission will become of great importance—and become global!

We would like to take this opportunity to give our most profound thanks to all who helped Operation Earth Light to become in all ways operational—and especially thank the original designer of the Apparatus.

Thank you, My son.

End of communication.

Babaji.

The following is an extract from a lengthy series of mental transmissions over several days between Dr King and advanced interplanetary beings. These transmissions were initiated by Dr King in order to help relieve a dangerous outbreak of fires in the Los Angeles area. The response to one of these fires—the Great Malibu Fire of 1993—"represented the largest mobilization of emergency resources within a one-two day period in the history of the United States," according to an official report by the County of Los Angeles Fire Department entitled "Old Topanga Incident." Miraculously, despite the ferocity and scale of these fires, the death toll was three and all the fires were contained within a few days. You will notice that in this exchange Dr King uses a designated code name, which he was not permitted to disclose.

Nixies Zero Zero Five and Nixies Zero Zero Nine, October 27 1993

Dr George King: This is (Code Name) to Nixies Zero Zero Five. Yes, Nixies Zero Zero Five, I am very ill this morning and am not up to par, but I want to make a manipulation to help the overall conditions and people helping to put these fires out, which are all around us here. As a matter of fact, I can see the smoke from here. Would you be available to help disperse any of our Prayer Power Energy?

Nixies Zero Zero Five: Yes, definitely. I will also bring other Agents in to help in this. I will start on that immediately.

When is your Energy going to be released?

Dr George King: Our Spiritual Energy Radiator is on at the moment with Energy from Space Power II [this refers to a mission in which the spiritual energy radiators are used to send energy to the world], but if I let go some Prayer Power Energy, it will trigger others from a Karmic point of view, like The Great White Brotherhood.

Nixies Zero Zero Five: Keep that Energy going until 11.00 a.m. and then put your Battery on and We will be ready to help disperse that Energy in a very significant manner. In the meantime, We will make sure that the Space Power II Energy is used most potently.

Dr George King: Thank You very much. This is (Code Name) closing down for the moment with Nixies Zero Zero Five.
(Pause)
Yes, Nixies Zero Zero Nine.

Nixies Zero Zero Nine: Yes, We too can help in this manipulation.

Dr George King: Thank You very much. This is (Code Name) closing down.

* * * * * * * * * *

Dr George King: This is (Code Name) to Nixies Zero Zero Five. We are about to place one of our Batteries on the air.

Nixies Zero Zero Five: That would be good. This will create a Karmic trigger.

Dr George King: How do You want us to do it?

Nixies Zero Zero Five: Sequential ... (classified information) ... until I let you know when to stop.

Dr George King: Fine. That will be on at 11.00 a.m. when our first run of Operation Space Power II has finished.

Thank You very much. This is (Code Name) standing by.

The Master Aetherius, January 7 1956

Keep your soul upwards, and know that the spirit is there—the spirit which is everything, the spirit which is pure God, in the highest phase, in the highest octave of manifestation, the spirit, oh men of Terra, that you are really. Don't look at your feet dear friends—don't look at your feet. Look above the top of your heads into real light. Don't you see that by doing that—even apart from looking for us—doing that, you are raising your consciousness? You are doing a physical action, you are taking your eyes away from the lower octaves of material existence, and raising them to the higher aspects of existence, by looking upwards, reaching upwards.

You know, a tiny little plant, if you put it in the darkness, it will send a tendril upwards towards the light—upwards and upwards and upwards will that tendril go. And then, when it reaches the light, verily will it blossom forth. You are the same, dear friends; you are like so many tiny little plants. Reach upwards to the light. Let the sun shine—metaphorically speaking—in your eyes, not on the nape of your necks.

Just before I go, let me just say this one thing please. What are you? You are the expression of life! You are all the expression of life! A tiny blade of grass is the expression of life, seeking experience, life. The same life, the same life that runs through rocks, through the sea, through grass, through trees, through you—it is the same life. It is seeking experience. It is like the tiny little tendril, reaching for the light, reaching for the light, so that it can blossom forth. And, when you have found this light, dear friends, you too will blossom forth, and great will be your joy.

You cannot now, at this moment, realize how happy you could be, if only you kept looking upwards, you kept your thoughts going upwards, you kept every atom of your power working upwards towards your own salvation. And what is that salvation? That salvation, dear friends, is the direct—the direct—the complete—the whole realization that within you is the spark of God Itself!

That is what you must do. Sooner or later you have to do it—every one of you has to do it. A blade of grass has to do it; a field mouse has to do it; a robin has to do it; a lion has to do it; an elephant has to do it; you have to do it. Every one of you, individually, collectively, have to do it!

Start it now: look upwards, send your mind upwards. Broaden your mind, broaden your consciousness. Let the mighty powers which come through the sky down to Earth, flow through you, let them flow through you. Then indeed will be your joy. Yes! Joy beyond any description; power beyond any description will be yours; Enlightenment beyond any description. Wisdom like a flower will blossom from the shells here, from the minds here, from the souls here, from the spirits here.

Thank you very much for your kind attention this evening. I have further work to do on another planet, so must go now.

There is an evidence-based case for UFOs and the extraterrestrial message, but unless we really want to know the answer, it won't matter to us anyway. I have attended conferences and provided information to researchers, which they accepted but were not interested enough to pursue. As the sixteenth-century French writer and philosopher Michel de Montaigne put it so devastatingly: "Once conform, once do what others do because they do it, and a kind of lethargy steals over all the finer senses of the soul." If you really want to know something, and you make the effort, at some point you will find out. If you are not really sure and you are happy to leave it there, so be it. If you think it is all a load of nonsense, good luck to you. Whatever conclusion any of us comes to, it will not alter the facts about UFOs and those who man them. That, too, is part of the extra-terrestrial message.

"We are all in the gutter, but some of us are looking at the stars" is a great quote but perhaps these words show more perspicacity than their author, Oscar Wilde, could have known. From ancient documents to the modern day, we have traced a consistent record of interaction between vehicles from space and our world, between cosmic visitors and the people of a wretchedly backward planet. Yes, this world can fairly be described as a gutter when you look at the greed, savagery, and materialistic indulgence that allow so many millions to live in squalor, disease, and poverty. And yes, we should look to the stars, for there lie our hope and salvation in the form of direct, cosmic intervention, through encounters, teachings, and missions to transform humanity.

If you were to ask me to recommend to you one book to help you to take this further, it would be my personal favorite, *The Nine Freedoms*, which contains an outstanding series of cosmic transmissions delivered by Mars Sector 6 in 1961, and a truly revelatory commentary upon them by Dr King. It was this book above all others that inspired me to take to the dedicated path of service through The Aetherius Society, which my wife and I and many of our friends have followed for years. For us, there is simply no greater privilege than cooperating directly with the Cosmic Masters and their plan for our world.

This is the transcript of a very rare question and answer session conducted on live television between the Master Aetherius, speaking through Dr King, and a group of questioners brought together by the BBC on May 21 1959. Dr King entered samadhic trance in front of studio lights and cameras, which was an extremely dangerous and, in view of that, a profoundly compassion-ate thing to do. The interview proceeded as follows:

The Master Aetherius: Good evening, my dear friends.

Questioner: Good evening. Your name is?

The Master Aetherius: I am known as—Aetherius.

Questioner: Where do you come from?

The Master Aetherius: The Planet Venus.

Questioner: Where are you speaking from now?

The Master Aetherius: I am sorry, my dear friend. I cannot answer that question for you.

Questioner: I had wondered simply whether you were in a Vehicle of some kind, a Space Ship described by Mr King when he was talking to me or whether you were in your normal abode, but you can't tell me that?

The Master Aetherius: No.

Questioner: You do travel normally, in what Mr King has described as Flying Saucers when you move about Space, do you?

The Master Aetherius: That is quite correct. We have indeed been visiting this Earth of yours for some eighteen million of your Earth years.

Questioner: When you come here, what is your purpose?

The Master Aetherius: At the moment, Earth as you call it, faces a certain situation. This situation can be described as rather a dangerous one. You are liable to upset the balance of your Earth through (i) Atomic Experimentation and (ii) your deviation from the Spiritual Laws.

Questioner: Are your visits designed to warn us against this?

The Master Aetherius: Yes.

Questioner: Can anybody see Flying Saucers when they arrive?

The Master Aetherius: Oh yes. The vehicles that you call Flying Saucers are quite physical. If you fired a 16-in. shell at the hull of a Flying Saucer, it would burst when it came into contact with the force screen or protective barrier round the Vessel.

Questioner: Is there one single message that you would like to give us this evening? I am afraid it must be brief. You will understand that.

The Master Aetherius: Yes. I would like to say this. If you are a Christian, then live the Laws as laid down by Jesus. If you are a Buddhist, live the Laws as laid down by Buddha. If you are a Hindu, then be the best Hindu. This procedure is the one true Way for men of Earth to save themselves from their lower aspects.

Questioner: Thank you, Aetherius, very much indeed. Good night.

The Master Aetherius: Good night.

INDEX